The Observers Series
POND LIFE

About the Book

This remarkably comprehensive book illustrates and describes briefly something of the almost incredible wealth and variety of plant and animal life in ponds and streams. Over 450 items are illustrated, and the pictorial keys have been planned to enable specimens to be identified to family or genus.

As with past editions, this book will be a valuable aid to anglers, whose success so often depends upon a good understanding of the habitat of their quarry.

About the Author

John Clegg was Curator of the Haslemere Educational Museum in Surrey from 1949 to 1962 and later of Torquay Natural History Museum and the Gilbert White Museum at Selborne, Hampshire. As a freelance writer and photographer he has always specialized in freshwater biology. His larger book, *Freshwater Life*, is also published by Frederick Warne. He is an Honorary Fellow of the Linnean Society and a Life Member of the Freshwater Biological Association. His home is now in Cumbria.

D1323049

The *Observer's* series was launched in 1937 with the publication of *The Observer's Book of Birds*. Today, fifty years later, paperback *Observers* continue to offer practical, useful information on a wide range of subjects, and with every book regularly revised by experts, the facts are right up-to-date. Students, amateur enthusiasts and professional organisations alike will find the latest *Observers* invaluable.

'Thick and glossy, briskly informative' – *The Guardian*

'If you are a serious spotter of any of the things the series deals with, the books must be indispensable' – *The Times Educational Supplement*

OBSERVERS

POND LIFE

John Clegg

Frederick Warne

FREDERICK WARNE
Published by the Penguin Group
27 Wrights Lane, London W8 5TZ, England
Viking Penguin Inc., 40 West 23rd Street, New York, New York 10010, U.S.A.
Penguin Books Australia Ltd, Ringwood, Victoria, Australia
Penguin Books Canada Ltd, 2801 John Street, Markham, Ontario, Canada L3R 1B4
Penguin Books (N.Z.) Ltd, 182–190 Wairau Road, Auckland 10, New Zealand

Penguin Books Ltd, Registered Offices: Harmondsworth, Middlesex, England

First published 1956
Second Edition 1967
Third Edition 1980
Fourth Edition 1986
3 5 7 9 10 8 6 4 2

Originally published as *The Observer's Book of
Pond Life* in small hardback format

ISBN 0 7232 3338 1

Printed and bound in Great Britain by
William Clowes Limited, Beccles and London

CONTENTS

PREFACE

In the thirty years which have elapsed since this book first appeared the study of pond life has changed in a number of ways, perhaps the most important being that the number of people indulging in the pursuit has increased immeasurably. Whereas the book was written originally with the amateur naturalist in mind, it is more likely now to be used by an increasing number of students from school or college as part of a field study course at one of the many outdoor pursuits centres in various parts of the country. However, an invasion of a pond by perhaps thirty or more students presents a totally different situation from that of one or two individual naturalists carrying out a leisurely study, and it is the author's earnest hope that organizers of such parties of students will minimize the pressure on ponds they study by following the procedures suggested in Part 4 of the Book, "Studying Pond Life" on pages 157 to 165.

The disappearance of many ponds throughout the country in recent years makes these procedures even more important. However, it is satisfactory to observe that the losses are to some extent being minimized by the care being taken by local amenity societies and county or regional nature conservation trusts to repair and restore existing ponds in their areas and even to create new ones.

The ease with which a new pond can be made using new pond-lining materials has enabled both individual gardeners and many schools to provide ponds in their grounds. This is a useful conservation exercise, for some groups of animals, such as frogs, newts and dragonflies, whose existence has been threatened by the disappearance of many of their natural habitats, readily colonize small artificial ponds. Help in starting and maintaining such ponds is available from many garden centres who now stock pond requisites; some nurseries specialize in this range of goods.

In this new edition of the book scientific names have again been brought up-to-date and a new book list prepared. The main purpose of the book is to provide a compact pictorial guide to common freshwater plants and animals, and the integration of text and illustrations should now facilitate identification.

Inevitably with such a vast number of organisms that can occur in even a small pond, it is quite impossible to include every one that might conceivably be found, but by carefully selecting typical representatives of all main groups for inclusion, it should be possible to identify the family, or even the genus, of a specimen from the illustrations, the pictorial keys and by the text description.

JOHN CLEGG
1985

ACKNOWLEDGEMENTS

Wherever possible, actual specimens, alive or preserved, have been used as subjects for illustrations. The author and publishers are, however, indebted to the following publishers and authors who have permitted the adaptation of illustrations appearing in their books or scientific papers: The Syndics of the Cambridge University Press, *A Treatise of the British Freshwater Algae* by the late G. S. West; The Ray Society, monographs on *British Hydracarina* by Soar and Williamson, *Aquatic (Naiad) Stage of the British Dragonflies* by W. J. Lucas, *Polyzoa* by G. J. Allman and *British Charophyta* by Groves and Bullock-Webster; the Royal Entomological Society, *Transactions*, Volume 91, Part 10, *The Taxonomy and Ecology of the Nymphs of British Plecoptera* by H. B. N. Hynes and various papers on the larvae of British Trichoptera by Dr N. E. Hickin; the Essex Field Club *Transactions*, Volume XXVI, for diagrams of *Asellus* by D. J. Scourfield; and to Messrs Wheldon and Wesley for the loan of a rare continental work on leeches.

The pictorial keys on pages 186–9 (**1, 459**) are adapted from one that illustrated an article by the late Mr L. C. Johnson in *School Science Review*, Volume XXVII, No. 102. Mr Johnson was also responsible for the dichotomous keys on pages 166–174.

The author is especially indebted to the series of Scientific Publications of the Freshwater Biological Association and to the other works listed in 'Books for Further Reading' on pages 175–6 which have been freely drawn upon in writing this book.

The illustrations in colour and line are by Gordon Riley, Eric D. Hollowday, R. B. Davis and the late Ernest C. Mansell. The photographs are by the author.

1. INTRODUCTION

Life In Fresh Water

Freshwater habitats are within reach of most of us. Ponds, lakes, streams, ditches, rivers, reservoirs, ornamental 'lakes' in city parks, even bird baths and rainwater butts, all provide fascinating material to observe and study. Each has its characteristic community or population of plants and animals, in many ways interdependent on one another.

The earliest kinds of plants and animals that occurred on the earth lived in water, and many millions of years elapsed before some kinds became adapted to live on dry land. Water, as a sphere of life, possesses many advantages, particularly for smaller creatures. Aquatic organisms, for instance, are less likely to meet that castastrophe which can so easily overtake a living thing on land—desiccation, or drying up.

The density of water too, supports delicate and fragile animals and plants and many forms are thus able to exist in water which would be quite incapable of living on land where they would have to support their own weight. Many minute kinds of both animals and plants called collectively *plankton* (Greek = drifting, roaming), which are so important in the economy of lakes and ponds, spend their whole existence floating about in the water.

This property of buoyancy, allied to the mobility of water, enables quite tiny creatures (and plants) to move about easily, even with such apparently feeble means of transport as the *cilia*, or lashing hairs, and the whip-like *flagella*, with which some of the lower forms of life are endowed.

On the surface of all water there is a layer called the *surface-film* which acts like a skin, supporting light objects which are on top of it and also capable of holding some specially adapted animals, such as gnat larvae, from its underside. This junction between the water and the atmospheric air is of great importance to many aquatic animals, particularly those that have to come to the surface to breathe.

Water is a poor conductor of heat and also takes a longer time to warm up or cool down than air. Generally speaking, therefore, *temperature* fluctuations are less violent in freshwater habitats than on land, which is an advantage to both animals and plants. The *transparency* of water enables light adequate for plant growth to penetrate all types of freshwater habitat except the deeper regions of some lakes and rivers.

Chemical Factors   Pure water would not maintain living organisms for long, but natural waters are almost always richly supplied with substances, both gases and solids, which have been dissolved in it. Of the gases, *oxygen* and *carbon dioxide* are the two most important. The former is obtained partly by being dissolved at the surface, where air meets water. Any violent agitation of the surface causes more air, and therefore more oxygen, to be dissolved, which explains why river water, splashing over stones as it moves along, is much better oxygenated than the still waters of a pond. Thus, as a rule, aquatic creatures that need a lot of oxygen for respiration are usually found in rivers. Oxygen, too, is given out by green plants during the hours of daylight when the process called photosynthesis is going on. In this process plants take in the gas carbon dioxide and, with the aid of water and sunlight, manufacture the carbohydrate part of their food. Oxygen is given off as a waste product, and in aquatic plants goes into solution in the water to augment the supply already there. On a bright, sunny day in summer, a weedy pond may in fact contain more oxygen than can readily be dissolved and it is then said to be supersaturated with oxygen.

Oxygen is a necessity for the existence of all living

things, both plant and animal, and where it is scarce, as for example in black evil-smelling ponds where the decomposition of decaying matter by bacteria has used most of it up, other living organisms may be absent altogether.

Most of the simpler aquatic animals absorb oxygen through the whole of their 'skin' by the process of diffusion, but others have special areas or organs such as gills where this diffusion can take place.

Carbon dioxide is the gas that is given off by animals in the process of respiration and as it dissolves fairly readily in water some of the supply there, which as we have seen is of importance to the plants in making their food, comes from the animals. But it is also obtained from water entering a pond or lake, and a reserve supply is maintained in all natural waters in the form of chemical substances called bicarbonates and carbonates which can give up their carbon dioxide under certain circumstances.

Other chemical substances which are important in water are nitrates, sulphates, chlorides, phosphates of various metals such as potassium, sodium, magnesium, calcium and iron, as well as soluble silica compounds. These are obtained by being dissolved out of the soil or mud on which the pond or lake is standing; from the decay of plant and animal remains; or by being washed into the water from the land. The presence or absence of these substances determines to a great extent the kinds of plants and animals that will be found in any particular stretch of water. Thus a poor supply of calcium salts will usually coincide with a scarcity or even complete absence of water snails, since these animals need calcium to build their shell. Similarly, water plants will generally be more abundant in waters rich in calcium, as for example on chalky soils.

Types of Freshwater Habitats

It may be as well to say a few words about the characteristics of the types of freshwater habitats that one may expect to encounter.

Ponds   Ponds are of many kinds but typically are small bodies of shallow, stagnant water in which rooted plants can grow even in the deepest parts. Water movements are slight and temperatures tend to fluctuate rather widely. The abundance of plants ensures that during the hours of daylight oxygen is plentiful but at night, with the cessation of photosynthesis and with the plants themselves taking in their normal supples of oxygen for respiration, the supply of oxygen may be very low indeed.

The characteristic animals of ponds are those that live on the bottom or among the plants—water beetles, water bugs, dragonfly nymphs, caddis larvae, and the like.

Streams and Rivers   These provide a habitat quite different from that of a pond. The flow of water prevents the growth of much plant life and necessitates modifications to the body structure of the animals to prevent their being carried away, such as the flattening of some mayfly nymphs. Oxygen is more abundant and temperatures are more constant. Stream creatures transferred to a still-water aquarium usually die fairly quickly because of the higher temperature and lack of oxygen in the water.

Rivers, of course, vary greatly in their conditions throughout their course—the swift, torrential waters of the upper reaches, the quieter flowing stretch on the plain, and the brackish area near the mouth all have their characteristic fauna and flora.

Lakes   Lakes are wide expanses of open water, with depths too great for higher plants to grow there. Exposed as they are to the full force of the wind, wave action, particularly on the shore, may be an important feature in determining the type of plants and animals that live in them. The lakes of the Lake District and Wales are typical examples, but the large artificial reservoirs now common in many parts of the country for town water supplies are true lakes in this sense. When lakes are on hard rocks, from which very few mineral salts can be dissolved, they have a very sparse plant and animal life; whereas on softer rocks, lakes usually have an abundance of both higher plants and minute plankton forms, and these in turn enable a wealth of animals to live in them. The first kind of lake is called an *unproductive lake* and the second a *productive lake*.

Primarily or secondarily aquatic?

In freshwater there are representatives of all the main groups of both plants and animals. Some of the commoner examples of each of these groups will be described in the pages that follow. It should be borne in mind, however, that although many, perhaps most of them, are *primarily aquatic organisms* in the sense that their ancestors have always lived in the water—there are a few groups containing a large number of individuals, that have only taken to the water late in their evolution. These, to which the term *secondarily aquatic* is given, include all the flowering plants, all the aquatic insects, mites, spiders and some of the water snails. If this fact is borne in mind, it will help sometimes to explain some peculiarity of structure or habit that is puzzling.

How to use this book for identification

Pictures of most of the species likely to be encountered are included in the text, but as a quick guide to the animals that can be seen at the pondside with a naked eye or hand lens, the keys on pages 186–9 may be helpful.

Naturally these cannot include all the kinds of creatures that may be found and the simplified descriptions may lead to some false trails, but the keys should cover most of the commoner groups that will occur.

Having found the main group to which the specimen belongs, the *Keys for the Identification of Selected Groups* which appear towards the end of this book, may enable a more precise identification to be made.

2. WATER PLANTS

Classification of the plant kingdom

Before dealing in more detail with the plants found in
aquatic habitats it will be as well to give a brief outline of
the way in which plants generally are classified.   Four
major groups of the plant kingdom are recognized, and
these are subdivided as follows:

1 THALLOPHYTA
   (i) Schizomycetes, the bacteria, of which some live in
fresh water.
   (ii) Algae, mainly aquatic plants, including the seaweeds and many freshwater kinds e.g. *Spirogyra*, the
diatoms, desmids, etc.
   (iii) Fungi, the toadstools, moulds, etc. Some aquatic
species.
2 BRYOPHYTA
These include the mosses and liverworts of which a few
species live in fresh water.
3 PTERIDOPHYTA
Sometimes called the vascular cryptogams, these include
ferns, horsetails and club-mosses and a few aquatic species.
4 SPERMATOPHYTA
These are the seed-bearing or flowering plants and
include many aquatic species. These will be discussed
first.

FLOWERING PLANTS

As the members of the last group—the seed plants or
flowering plants—are those which the observer will first
encounter in his expeditions, we will start with descriptions of these, leaving the other groups until later.
   The higher water plants do not belong to a single

family; representatives of many diverse families and natural orders are found in and around freshwater and seem to have taken to an aquatic habitat independently. As is only to be expected under such circumstances they exhibit varying stages of adaptation to their new environment. If the margins of a large pond, ditch or slow river are examined carefully it will be apparent that the plants are not growing haphazardly but are arranged in fairly definite zones correlated on the whole with depth of water and each forming a characteristic community (2). There is, it is true, a certain amount of intermingling but the following broad types of vegetation may usually be observed: the *marsh plants* growing in the relatively drier situation some distance from the water and not normally subject to flooding; the *swamp plants* either in the water or on the very edge; the species rooted in the shallow water but with *floating leaves*; the *free-floating* vegetation; and finally the *totally submerged* rooted plants, extending into the deeper water as far as the decreasing light permits (2).

Submerged Plants As might be expected, the last group of plants show the greatest adaptations. These are the true water plants, or *hydrophytes*, as they are termed. As we take them from the water we notice how limp and weak their stems and leaves are and how pale and translucent. They are quite unable to support themselves and if we were to examine their structure with a microscope we should find that they lack the woody tissue and tough fibres which land plants have to enable them to grow upwards to obtain light and air. Hydrophytes are supported all round by the water and have no need of such strengthening, which would in any case be a disadvantage, preventing them from adapting themselves to changes of water level or to water movements.

In land plants, the whole water supply required is usually provided through the roots and taken to all parts by a system of intercommunicating tubes. If we cut a shoot or flower and place the cut end in a vase of water it will keep fresh, perhaps for days, because water can still

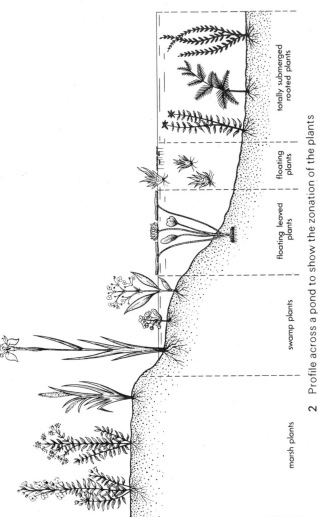

2 Profile across a pond to show the zonation of the plants

marsh plants | swamp plants | floating leaved plants | floating plants | totally submerged rooted plants

be carried to all the parts. In water plants, however, each portion of the plant absorbs directly what water it needs and a shoot or leaf removed from the pond wilts very quickly, even if its end is placed in water. With the water taken in by aquatic plants a good part of their food material is also included. In some alkaline or 'hard' waters the plants may have a chalky deposit on their stems and leaves. This demonstrates that they have obtained some of their requirements of the gas carbon dioxide from the soluble calcium bicarbonate in the water, and the insoluble calcium carbonate left has been deposited on the surface of the plant as a limy coating.

Totally submerged plants have no stomata or 'breathing pores' on their leaves but in those species such as water-lilies which have floating leaves, they are present on the upper surface only. To operate successfully the stomata must not get choked with water and in such plants the upper surface of the leaf may be waxy so that water collects in globules and soon rolls off (**3**).

Most of the true water plants are perennials and the problem of tiding over the winter has been solved in a number of different ways. Some such as water starwort

3 Leaves of white water-lily: waxy surface repelling water

4 Bladderwort

(7) and water soldier (**18**) merely sink to the warmer water at the bottom of the pond and remain there until spring. A number, which include frogbit, water milfoil (8) and bladderwort (**4**), produce in the autumn special tightly-packed buds, filled with food material. When the parent plant decays these turions, or 'winter buds' (**5**), break loose and sink to the mud. In spring some of the food material is used up and the turions float to the surface to give rise to new plants. Water-lilies and the pondweeds, *Potamogeton*, store up reserve food material in swollen stems or rhizomes buried in the mud. From these, new shoots arise in spring.

5 Winter buds of frogbit:
stages of development in the spring

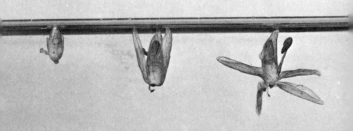

6 Canadian pondweed

One of the best known of the totally submerged plants is Canadian pondweed (**6**), *Elodea canadensis*. It was introduced from North America in about 1840 and has established itself in most parts of Britain. It illustrates in a striking manner a feature common in hydrophytes: that multiplication by vegetative means is more common than by the setting of seed. For many years only the female plant was known in Britain and its rapid spread, now happily checked, was due to the ease with which small fragments, broken off the brittle stems, grew into new plants. The minute lilac flowers, which are usually overlooked, are borne on extremely long and slender stalks.

Of the water milfoils the commonest species are *Myriophyllum spicatum* (**8**) and *M. verticillatum*. Their long stems bear large numbers of dissected leaves borne in whorls (four leaves to a whorl in *M. spicatum*, five to a whorl in *M. verticillatum*) and terminate in a short spike of small flowers, the male and female parts being borne in separate flowers, although both kinds of flowers are found on the same plant. In *M. verticillatum* the flower-spikes are long, and the flowers are in axillary whorls; in *M. spicatum* the flowers are on a leafless spike.

Hornwort, *Ceratophyllum demersum* (**9**), is one of the most completely adapted of all our plants to aquatic life as it flowers and pollinates under water. The male and female flowers appear in late summer; they are separate, although borne on the same plant, and grow inconspicuously in the axils of the leaves. Although at times pale shoots called rhizoids are developed which anchor the plant in the mud, this plant has no true roots and often

Submerged plants

floats freely, but erect, in the water. The related *C. submersum* has lighter-coloured leaves which are thrice-forked, whereas in the previous species they are only once or twice-forked.

The water starworts, *Callitriche* (7), are plants in which it is difficult to identify the individual species as such differences as there are, appear mainly in the fruits. Their bright green foliage with the star-shaped terminal rosette of leaves from which their name in derived is to be seen in all waters, even in cart-ruts and similar unpromising situations.

The lovely lilac flowers of water violet, *Hottonia palustris* (10), are to be sought appearing above the surface of still ditches and drainage dykes. The dissected leaves are much broader than those of both hornwort or the milfoils with which this plant is sometimes confused by the uninitiated. Distribution somewhat local; flowers in May and June.

The water crowfoots, *Ranunculus* spp. (11), which make such a brave show with their white starry flowers on ponds and ditches in spring, comprise a number of species which are also difficult to identify. The underwater leaves are divided into narrow segments but some of the species produce also flat, lobed, floating leaves. The pretty white blossoms with centres of yellow stamens appear in May and June and rise above the water, but after flowering the stalk curves downwards and the fruit is ripened below the surface.

Floating Plants   We have seen that in some hydro-phytes, as for example, hornwort, the 'roots' serve as an anchor rather than a source of nutrition. Certain species, frequenters of still waters, do not anchor themselves at all but float freely in the water.

The bladderworts, *Utricularia* (4), one of our three groups of carnivorous plants, have dispensed with roots and their long stems float horizontally in the water. The leaves are divided into hair-like segments on which are borne bladder-like traps that catch and digest the prey.

The duckweeds float at the surface with their roots hanging down into the water. They seem to grow best where there is a fairly high content of organic matter, and are therefore found in ponds, ditches and still waters. Lesser duckweed, *Lemna minor* (**12**), is a very common and widely distributed plant on still waters throughout Britain. The fronds are between 1·5 and 4·00 mm in diameter, flat and each bearing a single root. Great duckweed, *L. polyrrhiza* (**13**), grows in ditches and ponds but is local in distribution. The fronds are up to 10 mm in diameter, usually purplish in colour underneath and each bearing several roots. Gibbous duckweed, *L. gibba* (**15**), grows in still waters but is also rather local. The fronds are slightly larger than *L. minor*, convex on the upper surface and much swollen below except in winter. Ivy-leaved duckweed, *L. trisulca* (**16**), is common in ponds and ditches and the fronds are submerged.

Water fern, *Azolla filiculoides* (**14**), was introduced from North America as an aquarium plant, but it has now become naturalized in many places, particularly in the south. In autumn the plant turns red.

The true hydrophytes merge imperceptibly into plants which possess floating leaves, the upper surface of which is in contact with the air, and through which gaseous interchange can take place. Compared with the submerged ones these leaves are usually tough, to withstand the effects of wind and rain, and as we have seen, they are able to repel water to prevent their getting waterlogged.

The frogbit, *Hydrocharis morsus-ranae* (**5**, **17**), often covers the surface of ponds and ditches with its clusters of heart-shaped leaves and delicate white flowers. From its long runners, growing off in all directions, new plants arise so that in a short time a solid mat is formed. It is common except in the north, Cornwall and Ireland and flowers in July and August.

Water soldier, *Stratiotes aloides* (**18**), too, once established soon chokes a stretch of water. All the plants in Britain are female so no seed is set, and the prolific growth is due to the development of new plants at the end of runners.

Floating and floating-leaved plants

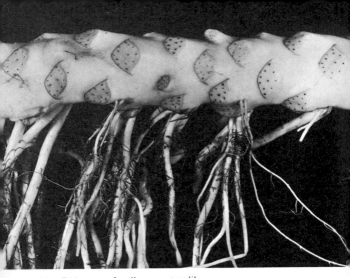

21 Rhizome of yellow water-lily

22 Fringed water-lily

Water soldier rises to the surface about June, to flower, but at other times floats deeper in the water. It is a rather local plant as it prefers calcareous waters.

The group of rooted plants with floating leaves include our two most lovely water plants, the yellow and white water-lilies. The white water-lily, *Nymphaea alba* (**19**), is fairly common and widely distributed in larger ponds and lakes. The yellow water-lily, *Nuphar lutea* (**20**, **21**), grows in ponds and lakes and also in canals, streams and ditches in most parts of Britain.

Resembling a water-lily, but not related to them, is an attractive plant of local distribution, the fringed water-lily, *Nymphoides peltata* (**22**). Its roundish leaves and its yellow flowers with fringed petals make it an attractive plant for a small garden pool.

The pondweeds, *Potamogeton*, are a large family and many members are difficult to identify, particularly as some of them hybridize. Perhaps the commonest is the floating pondweed, *Potamogeton natans*, whose large oval floating leaves form such a blanket on some ponds. Finally, amphibious bistort, *Polygonum amphibium* (**23**), is a frequent member of this community. Although it normally grows in the shallows of ponds, canals and slow rivers, there is a terrestrial form which thrives on the drier banks by the water. It is common and widely distributed.

Swamp Plants Forming a link between the last group and those that belong to what is usually known as the reedswamp community, is the bog bean, *Menyanthes trifoliata*, the floating rhizomes of which grow out from the bank, sometimes forming a thick mat. The three-lobed leaves and the upright raceme of white flowers tinged with pink, make it an attractive plant in spring before many of the other marginal plants are in evidence. The typical members of the reed swamp community, however, are tall, narrow-leaved plants, offering little resistance to the water and in consequence less likely to be damaged by floods. Their height ensures that changes of water level will not seriously interfere with their photosynthesis and

23

24

their tough fibres and hollow structure enable them to stand up to severe buffeting by wind without breaking.

Such a plant is the common reed, *Phragmites australis* (**27**). It grows to a height of 3 m and frequently forms dense reed beds around the margins of large bodies of water. It does not, however, grow well in acid or poor habitats. It is characteristic of such members of the reedswamp community that if undisturbed by man they have a tendency to encroach on the water area and in time they may even convert quite large sheets of water into marshes. Most of them send out creeping rhizomes from which new plants arise at intervals and it is a common sight to see rows of young reeds or reedmace plants advancing right out into the middle of a lake or large pond. Their lower parts limit water movements and encourage the accumulation of silt, while their death and decay in autumn continues the process. Their remains pile up year after year and so raise the level of the ground.

Three plants which have somewhat similar tall strap-

25　　　　　26　　　　27

shaped leaves are the yellow flag, *Iris pseudacorus* (**24**),
found in swampy places, the sweet flag, *Acorus calumus*,
and the branched bur-reed, *Sparganium erectum* (**26**), which
is common and widely distributed at the margins of
ponds, ditches and rivers. They are not related, however,
and can be distinguished even when not in flower by the
leaves. Those of the bur-reed are shorter and narrower
than the others, and three-sided at the base. The leaves of
sweet flag are of a lighter green than those of yellow flag,
crinkled at the edge and give off a delightful aromatic
odour when bruised; for this reason they were formerly
strewn over the floors of churches and castles.

The bulrush, *Typha latifolia* (**25**), often called the
reedmace, is a familiar and handsome member of the
reedswamp community. It is found at the margins of
ponds, lakes and river throughout Britain. Its great
flower-stems, up to 2·5 m high, bear at their ends the
cylindrical mass of female flowers, and above them,
without any space between, a smaller mass of male

27

flowers. The smaller *T. angustifolia* has a gap between the male and the female flowers. After fertilization has taken place there may be some 250,000 seeds on a single head of average size of the larger species.

The beautiful flowering rush, *Butomus umbellatus* (**28**), is one of our loveliest waterside plants. The umbel of pretty rose-pink blossoms is carried at the top of a long scape, or stalk, about 1 m high. It is found locally at the margins of rivers, ponds and ditches. The name is unfortunate for the plant is not related to the rushes.

The erect arrow-shaped leaves from which the arrow-head, *Sagittaria sagittifolia* (**30**), gets its name, are decorative additions to this zone; but the plant can also have long strap-shaped leaves under water and oval floating leaves. To the same family belongs the water-plantain, *Alisma plantago-aquatica* (**29**), a common plant with broad leaves, tapering to a point at the top, and a large, much-branched compound panicle of small white flowers. It is widely distributed at the edges of ponds, ditches and slow rivers. Finally the lovely marsh marigold, *Caltha palustris* (**31**), brings a touch of sunshine when its gay yellow sepals are mirrored in the water in early spring.

28   29

30 Arrowhead

31 Marsh marigold

The Marsh Plants Away from the water's edge is a wealth of tall and beautiful plants. characterized by lush growth, often large leaves (since loss of moisture by transpiration is no problem in such damp surroundings), and a spongy structure with many hollow cavities in which can be stored air to make up for a possible lack of it in the wet soil. Here may be found the great water dock, *Rumex hydrolapathum*, rising up to 2 m high, with flat leaves often 1 m in length; the great willow-herb, or codlins-and-cream, *Epilobium hirsutum*, with its rose coloured flowers; purple loosestrife, *Lythrum salicaria*; meadow sweet, *Filipendula ulmaria*, and many more equally delightful species forming a fringe to the pond or stream.

Plants in a River The amount of plant life in running water varies considerably with the type of river and the rate or flow at any particular place. In rapid streams such as those in the north and west, the current is too great to permit smaller particles of silt to accumulate and thus the river bed is too stony to allow rooted plants to establish themselves.

The gentler rivers of the south, on the contrary, often have considerable silted regions, and particularly on the chalk streams, plant growth may be so abundant that weed-cutting becomes a necessary and frequent operation to prevent the flow being choked. The presence of fairly large amounts of calcium in the water (a condition, incidentally, which is not restricted to chalk streams), and also of organic silt in moderation encourages plant growth, but too much organic matter—as for instance, in a river polluted with industrial waste or untreated sewage—may have the opposite effect with serious repercussions on the animal life.

Light, too, is an important factor in influencing the growth of plants in a river. Even clear water absorbs a certain amount of light passing through it and where the water is cloudy, as it is in some lowland rivers, there may be no plants on the river bed at all.

As in still waters, the plants in a river trap silt around

their lower parts and if allowed to grow in abundance this may raise the level of the river bed, or even form islands. Conditions are formed in these silted regions for the establishment of a distinct community of plants which might include water starwort (7), Canadian pondweed, various-leaved pondweed, *Potamogeton gramineus*, and even the yellow water-lily (**20, 21**).

In the swifter regions of a lowland river, where the bed is mainly stony, a few plants can root in the silt trapped between the stones. Here may be found river water-crowfoot, *Ranunculus fluitans*, lesser water-parsnip, *Berula erecta*, fool's water-cress, *Apium nodiflorum*, and willow moss, *Fontinalis antipyretica* (**95**).

On the really rapid or torrential streams, the only visible plants are mosses which are securely anchored to the stones, such as water moss and *Eurhynchium riparioides*. Nevertheless these are important in providing shelter for characteristic groups of small animals.

For one of the most important features of plants in any aquatic habitat is as a shelter for the animals—shelter from enemies, from light and, in a river, from the ceaseless current. Other valuable features of plants are, of course, as food for the herbivorous animals, supports in which eggs can be laid and aerators of the water.

FLOWERLESS PLANTS

The members of the first three groups of the plant kingdom mentioned on page 14—Thallophyta (bacteria, algae and fungi), Bryophyta (mosses and liverworts) and Pteridophyta (ferns, horsetails and club-mosses) include a vast assemblage of plants and in this book there will be space to mention only a very few of those which will be most commonly encountered.

BACTERIA AND FUNGI

These are the natural agents for bringing about the decay and decomposition of dead plant and animal material both on land and in water. Without them the world would be piled up with dead bodies. Lacking chlorophyll, the green colouring matter with which green plants manufacture their food materials from the inorganic substances carbon dioxide and water, most bacteria and fungi must get their sustenance ready-made either from dead animals or plants (when they are termed *saprophytic*) or from live ones (when they are *parasitic*). They break down organic material by the use of enzymes.

The bacteria found naturally in freshwater are, in general, beneficial, and by breaking down the complex organic materials in the remains of dead animals and plants into simpler chemical substances which can be used again by plants, they help to keep the food supply in circulation.

Some of the fungi, however, are not so beneficial. Water-moulds such as *Saprolegnia* (32), for example, attack living fishes, entering the skin where there has been some slight wound or loss of scales, to produce the white fluffy fungus growth familiar to those who have kept goldfish in garden pools. The moulds also attack fish eggs when they are incubating, while others are parasitic on plants, including diatoms and other algae, and may sometimes be important in controlling their increase.

Both bacteria and fungi reproduce by means of spores, which are exceedingly minute and are produced in immense numbers. They spread by wind or water currents

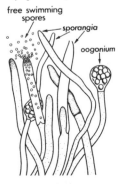

free swimming spores

sporangia

oogonium

32 Reproduction of *Saprolegnia*

and so are present everywhere, ready to give rise to new plants when conditions are suitable.

Like all living things, bacteria and fungi consume oxygen and thus in waters or mud containing much decaying material, this gas may be very scarce or even absent through their activities. Some bacteria, however, live without *free* oxygen, obtaining their supply from the breakdown of other substances. These *anaerobic* bacteria produce the characteristically obnoxious smell of the mud of polluted waters.

ALGAE

Classification of algae

Class	Freshwater examples
CYANOPHYTA, blue-green algae	*Nostoc, Anabaena*
CHRYSOPHYTA, yellow-green algae	*Vaucheria, Tribonema*, diatoms
CHLOROPHYTA, green algae	*Spirogyra, Volvox,* desmids
PHAEOPHYTA, brown algae (mostly marine)	
RHODOPHYTA, red algae (mostly marine)	*Batrachospermum*

The most familiar example of an alga is the green powdery growth on tree trunks and wooden posts, consisting of immense numbers of the cells of *Pleurococcus*. Most algae, however, are aquatic plants, the great majority living in the sea, where the larger species are known to us as seaweeds. There are nevertheless a bewildering number in freshwater, ranging from microscopic single-celled species, to the stoneworts, comparable in size and form to the higher plants. Some kinds have special reproductive cells or organs, while in others the same cells may fulfil both reproductive and vegetative functions.

All algae contain the green pigment chlorophyll and carry out the processes of nutrition in a similar way to higher water plants. This does not mean to say, however, that they are all of a uniform green colour for in some groups the pigment is masked by other pigments so that it is possible to classify algae into various groups based on their colour difference, which are correlated also with other important differences in development and life history.

Blue-green algae The blue-greens are the simplest forms and have a distinctive cell structure with no organized nucleus and no chloroplasts (or specialized pigment bodies), the colour being diffused over the cells. They occur in gelatinous masses, in filaments, or as single cells, and often become sufficiently abundant in late summer as to form a scum, or 'water-bloom' on the surface of the lakes or ponds. *Coelosphaerium* (**38**), *Microcystis* (**40**), *Aphanizomenon* and *Anabaena* (**35**) are among the genera which cause these 'water-blooms'.

Although there are several hundred species of blue-green algae we have had to select only seven for illustration here.

Nostoc (**33, 34**), of which 16 species are known to occur in Britain includes some terrestrial species. They occur as jelly-like masses, some attached to stones or among mosses in streams, others floating freely in the water.

Anabaena (**35**) is closely related to *Nostoc*, but usually found without a gelatinous sheath and the filaments are more rigid and less contorted. Commonly found in lakes and ponds. 12 species.

Rivularia (**37**), of which there are 4 species, is sometimes found attached to stones in mountain streams while

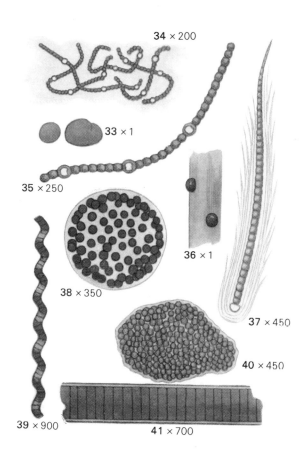

34 × 200

33 × 1

35 × 250

36 × 1

38 × 350

37 × 450

40 × 450

39 × 900

41 × 700

Blue-green algae

35

R. minutula occurs as roundish masses on plant stems (**36**).

Coelosphaerium (**38**) is a common genus in the plankton of lakes and large ponds. 4 species.

Spirulina (**39**) has filaments which are slender and twisted into a spiral. 3 species, one of which is common in still waters.

Microcystis (**40**) occurs in irregular shaped gelatinous masses in which the cells are closely packed. The colour varies from blue-green to rose-purple. 12 species.

Oscillatoria (**41**), of which there are 20 British species, can occur as floating masses, often mixed with mud particles, on the surface of ponds and ditches.

Green algae This is the largest group of freshwater algae and includes very diverse plants showing varying degrees of complexity of structure. Many are simple, single cells, some are groups of cells sometimes with a gelatinous covering, others are in the form of hollow spheres, flat plates, or filaments of cells joined end to end. The filaments may be branched or unbranched and in one group, the so-called siphon algae, resemble long open tubes.

The genus *Chlorella* is an example of the *single-celled* type. Occasionally it is present in a pond in such numbers as to colour the water green. Its great interest to the biologist, however, is that some of the species live in the bodies of various aquatic animals such as the freshwater sponges, the green Hydra and the single-celled animal *Stentor* (**115**), imparting to them a green colour. It is believed that both parties to this symbiotic partnership benefit, the alga obtaining carbon dioxide and perhaps other waste products from its host, and the latter, a richer supply of oxygen from the photosynthetic activity of the alga.

Volvox (**46, 49**), three species of which are found in Britain, is one example of an algae colony in the form of a hollow sphere. The individual units of the colony each bear two whip-like flagellae, the constant beating of which propels the colony through the water. Inside the sphere, daughter colonies are usually visible which eventually break free. *Volvox* is notoriously erratic in its occurrence; some years it will be so abundant in a pond as to make the water green, whereas in other years no trace of it can be found.

The *unbranched filamentous species* are perhaps the best known freshwater algae, as some of them form large floating masses in the water which are readily seen by the most casual observer.

Branched filaments are found in *Cladophora* (**55**, **56**), *Chaetophora* (**52**, **53**) and *Draparnaldia* (**54**), and also in the siphon alga *Vaucheria* (**71**).

Smaller green algae

Apart from *Volvox*, which is just visible to the naked eye, the algae described here can be seen only with the aid of a microscope. They are free-floating or move through the water by means of cilia.

Chlamydomonas (**42**) is usually found in ponds and ditches. 20 species.

Pandorina (**43**) is common and widely distributed in ponds and ditches.

Eudorina (**44**) occurs in the plankton of lakes, as well as in smaller bodies of water, being particularly abundant in autumn.

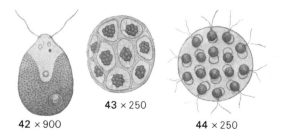

43 × 250

42 × 900

44 × 250

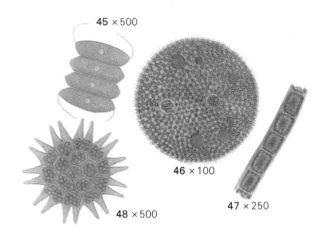

45 ×500

46 ×100

47 ×250

48 ×500

49 *Volvox aureus* ×34 (left a nauplius larva of a crustacean, *Diaptomus*)

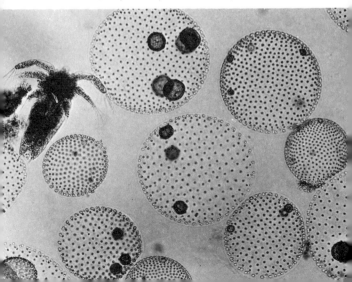

Scenedesmus (**45**) is common in the plankton of still waters. 12 species.

Volvox (**46, 49**) is one of the most beautiful microscopic objects in freshwater. 3 species of which *V. globator* is the largest.

Pediastrum (**48**) is most commonly found in ponds and ditches among water plants, but sometimes members of this genus occur in the plankton. 8 species.

Larger green algae   These are the most conspicuous of the algae for they frequently occur in large masses, floating on the surface of the water in spring and summer.

Microspora (**47**) is widely distributed and found usually in ponds, small stagnant pools, and drinking troughs.

Oedogonium (**50**, female filament with dwarf male attached) is found in floating masses in still waters. About 80 species.

Ulothrix (**51**) is common in ponds and ditches, occurring as bright green masses. 7 species.

Chaetophora (**52, 53**) may occur with a gelatinous branched plant body as illustrated, or in globular green masses an inch of more in diameter, usually in running water.

Draparnaldia (**54**) occurs as long pale green gelatinous filaments in clear waters. 2 species.

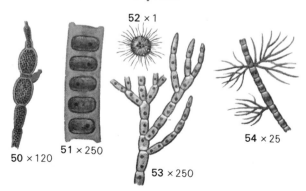

52 × 1

50 × 120

51 × 250

53 × 250

54 × 25

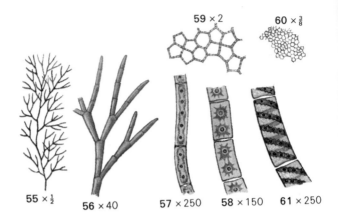

59 × 2   60 × ⅜

55 × ½   56 × 40   57 × 250   58 × 150   61 × 250

Cladophora (**55, 56**) numbers 3 species, one of which is free-floating in still waters, and two grow attached to stones.

Mougeotia (**57**) numbers 15 species, some of which are very abundant in lakes, ponds and ditches.

Zygnema (**58**) numbers 12 species and is common in ponds and ditches.

Water-net, *Hydrodictyon*, (**59, 60**) has cells which form a free-floating bag-like network up to 20 cm long.

Spirogyra (**61**) occurs as green floating masses in ponds and ditches. Slimy to the touch. 25 species.

Desmids are single-celled green algae; some are free-floating and others are found attached to larger plants. There are very many kinds and they are particularly common in pools in sphagnum bogs. They multiply asexually by the cell dividing at the part where it narrows, but occasionally there is a sexual conjugation where two cells merge and their contents unite to form a zygospore, usually globular in shape and bearing spines; from this one or more new desmids arise.

Spirotaenia (**62**) is a somewhat uncommon desmid found mainly in peat-bogs. 14 species.

Euastrum (**63**), some of whose 44 species are widely distributed, is sometimes found among *Sphagnum*.

Penium (**64**) numbers 16 species.

Cosmarium (**65**) is a very large genus with about 250 British species. Some are found in ponds and ditches, but the majority occur in bog pools.

Cylindrocystis (**66**) occurs in peat pools and often among *Sphagnum*. 5 species.

Staurastrum (**67**) is another large genus with about 160 species in Britain. Most occur in the mountainous parts of the country, and some are found in the plankton of lakes.

Closterium (**68**) is probably the best-known genus of desmid with a characteristic curved cell. 62 species, some of which are common in ponds.

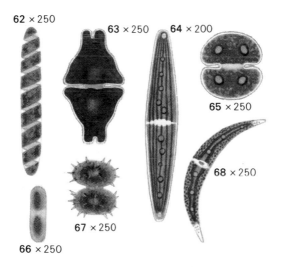

62 × 250

63 × 250   **64** × 200

65 × 250

67 × 250

66 × 250

68 × 250

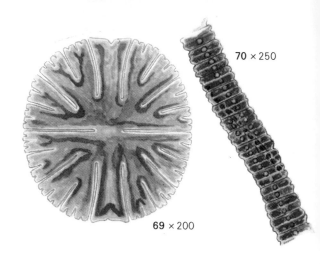

70 × 250

69 × 200

Micrasterias (**69**) includes some of the largest desmids among its number. The cells are typically almost circular or broadly elliptical in shape. 16 species, mainly found in bog pools.

Desmidum (**70**), the cells of which are joined together to form filaments, numbers 8 species, none of which is common.

Yellow-green algae The yellow-green pigment from which this group of algae derive their name is not immediately visible and the examples mentioned below appear green.

Vaucheria (**71**), showing reproductive organs, left: antheridium (male); right: oogonium (female), forms dense mats of compacted filaments in water or on damp ground.

Tribonema (**72**) is common, particularly in shady pools. 6 species.

Botrydium (**73, 74**) occurs on drying mud. 1 species.

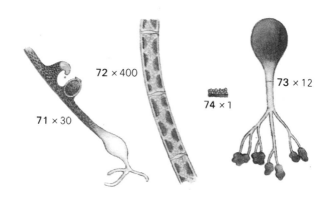

72 × 400

71 × 30

74 × 1

73 × 12

Yellow-green algae

Diatoms These exquisitely beautiful single-celled plants are very numerous in all waters. Unlike other plants the cell-wall is composed largely of the hard, flinty material, silica, and its surfaces are sculptured with fine lines, pits or projections. In living diatoms the full beauty of these markings is somewhat obscured but with suitable preparation they can be appreciated to the full under a medium power of the microscope.

Some diatoms are free floating, either singly or in groups and form a most important part of the plankton of lakes; others are attached to plants or stones and, as a brownish slimy coating, may be observed with the naked eye.

The individual diatom can be likened to a minute glass box with a deep lid, similar in construction to a pill-box or date-box. The top and bottom of the box are called the valves and the sides the girdle, and some care is needed in examining diatoms under the microscope to ascertain which part is under observation, as naturally the appearance will vary greatly in each case. Reproduction

43

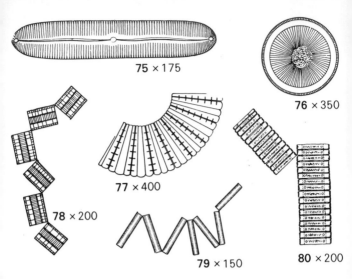

75 × 175

76 × 350

77 × 400

78 × 200

79 × 150

80 × 200

is effected by the two parts of the box separating and each then growing the missing portion, but occasionally two individuals merge together to produce an auxospore which develops into a new diatom.

Navicula (**75**) is widely distributed and particularly abundant in bog pools. 80 species.

Melosira (**76**) is usually found in long filaments and abundant in ponds, ditches and slow moving rivers. 8 species.

Meridion (**77**) has individual frustules which are united to form fan-shaped or spiral filaments, floating freely in stagnant water. 1 species.

Tabellaria (**78**) forms zig-zag filaments attached to plants. 2 species.

Diatoma (**79**) also forms zig-zag filaments and is common in still waters. 4 species.

Fragilaria (**80**) whose rectangular frustules are joined together into long ribbons is common and widely distributed. 5 species.

44

Asterionella (**81**), the frustules of which are usually joined by their bases to form star-shaped colonies, is very abundant in lakes, ponds and ditches. 2 species.

Cocconeis (**82**) is common and often found attached to water plants, including filamentous algae. 2 species.

Surirella (**83**) is common in the plankton of lakes. 8 species.

Eunotia (**84**) is found sometimes in chains, but also solitary or attached in clusters to algae.

Synedra (**85**) is a very common genus and widely distributed. 10 species.

Gomphonema (**86**) is often attached by mucilage stalks to plants or other supports. It is common and widely distributed. 14 species.

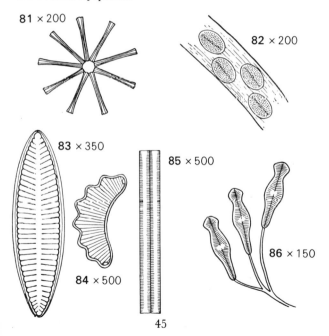

81 × 200

82 × 200

83 × 350

84 × 500

85 × 500

86 × 150

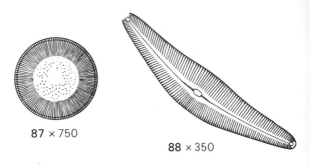

87 × 750

88 × 350

Cyclotella (**87**) is widely distributed and often abundant in the plankton of lakes. 6 species.

Cymbella (**88**) is found either free or attached by stalks to various supports, including wet rocks, on which they may form a light brown scum. 15 species.

Red algae In spite of the name of this group, this freshwater example may be purplish or even blue-green in colour.

Frog spawn alga, *Batrachospermum* (**89**, **90**) is found attached to stones in running water and, more rarely, in ponds.

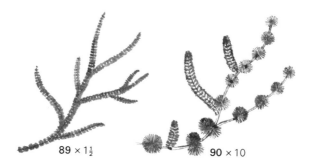

89 × 1½

90 × 10

91 × 10

92 × 1

94 × 10

93 × ½

Stoneworts These much larger and more complex plants are sometimes included in the green algae, but mainly because of their highly specialized reproduction, some authorities consider that they merit a separate division of the plant kingdom—Charophyta. There are over 30 species in Britain and they are classified into two main groups: the Nitelleae (**93, 94**) the members of which have forked branchlets, and the Chareae (**91, 92**) with unforked branchlets. The name stonewort refers to the brittle nature of the plants and the frequent presence of a limy coating on the surface of them.

Stonewort, *Chara vulgaris* (**92**); reproductive bodies (**91**), oogonium (above), antheridium (below).

Stonewort, *Nitella flexilis* (**93**); reproductive bodies (**94**), antheridium (below), oogonium (above).

MOSSES, LIVERWORTS AND FERNS

The remaining groups of flowerless plants are not well represented in fresh water. Long strands of willow moss, *Fontinalis antipyretica* (95) up to a metre in length, occur in both still and running water, but spore capsules are only produced when the plant is stranded above water-level.

The most abundant of the mosses are the various species of bog moss, *Sphagnum*, which occur in soft masses at the margins of some ponds and streams, and indeed in the water itself. The vast deposits of peat which occur in some parts of the country are formed largely from the decayed remains of immense accumulations of bog mosses. The plants are very absorbent of water owing to the presence of cells empty of protoplasm between the normal cells making up their structure; these serve merely for absorption and storage of moisture. Thus, even when the pool around which the mosses are growing dries up, the soft carpet of vegetation at the margin may still be boggy.

Several species of mosses are found encrusting stones in rapid streams or at the edges of waterfalls and as they are the only form of vegetation in such situations they provide

95 Willow moss

shelters for a specialized community of protozoa, rotifers and insects. Water feather moss, *Eurhynchium riparioides* is one of the largest and showiest of these and it is common on rocks and banks beside streams and waterfalls.

Of the liverworts, the great scented liverwort, *Conocephalum conicum*, so called because when bruised it gives off a pleasant smell, is widely distributed on wet rocks and walls at the margins of streams. Other liverworts represented in such situations are species of *Lunularia*, *Marchantia* and *Pellia*.

Floating crystalwort, *Riccia fluitans*, a liverwort, is usually found floating just below the surface of ponds and ditches, but it can also grow on wet mud. It is, in fact, when growing under the latter conditions that the plant is most likely to fruit. The form differs somewhat in the two different habitats; when floating, the plant is slender and green all over and possesses no rhizoids, or root-like growths. When growing on wet mud, on the other hand, the plant is thicker, usually has a violet tinge and develops rhizoids.

Quillwort, *Isoetes lacustris* (**96**), pillwort, *Pilularia globulifera*, water fern or fairy moss, *Azolla filiculoides* (**14**), and

96 Quillwort

the water horsetail, *Equisetum fluviatile*, are the only aquatic representatives of the fern-like plants (Pteridophyta) in this country.

Quillwort grows submerged in lakes and tarns of northern Britain, the water of which is poor in dissolved salts. It is a relic of an ancient group of plants which was abundant in earlier geological times. The quill-shaped leaves, from which the plant gets its name, twelve to twenty in number and about 150 mm long, all spring direct from the base of the plant in a rosette.

Pillwort grows at the margins of lakes and bog pools either submerged in the shallow water or on the damp ground nearby. Although widely distributed and not uncommon it is usually passed over as a grass. The leaves, which are about 75 mm long, arise from a creeping threadlike rootstock on which, and at the base of the leaves, are the 'pills'—the spore-containing bodies called, properly, sporocarps, from which the plant derives its name. They are spherical bodies, brown in colour, covered with hairs and about the size of a peppercorn. They are found from June to August.

Azolla filiculoides (**14**), a native of North America, has been naturalized in many parts of southern England. It is a floating plant with very attractive, deeply lobed leaves or fronds, borne on much-branched stems. The leaves are green in summer but towards autumn they develop rich reddish tints. A blue-green alga *Anabaena* (**35**) lives in cavities in the leaves.

Another species of *Azolla*, *A. caroliniana*, a native of western America, has also been introduced into Britain and the two species have probably often been confused. *A. caroliniana* is a much smaller plant with less dense branching. It lies flat on the surface of the water whereas *A. filiculoides* tends to grow in tufts which often protrude from the water surface. The roots of *A. caroliniana* are neither as numerous nor as conspicuous as in the larger species. *A. filiculoides* is said to fruit readily in Europe.

3. THE ANIMAL LIFE OF FRESH WATER

Classification of freshwater animal life

Subkingdom: PROTOZOA. Single-celled animals
    Class *MASTIGOPHORA. (FLAGELLATA)*.
  Euglena, Ceratium, etc.
    Class *RHIZOPODA (SARCODINA) Amoeba*,
    Actinophrys
    Class *SPOROZOA*. Parasitic protozoa
    Class *CILIOPHORA. Paramecium, Vorticella*
Subkingdom: METAZOA. Cellular animals
  Phylum **PORIFERA.** Sponges
  Phylum **COELENTERATA.**
    Class *HYDROZOA.* Hydras
  Phylum **PLATYHELMINTHES**. Flatworms
    Class *TURBELLARIA*
      Order Rнавросоеla. *Dalyellia*
      Order Tricladida. *Planaria*
    Class *TREMATODA*. Parasitic flatworms
    Class *CESTODA*. Parasitic flatworms
  Phylum **ROTIFERA**. *Brachionus*
  Phylum **GASTROTRICHA.** Hairy backs
  Phylum **NEMATODA.** Threadworms
  Phylum **NEMATOMORPHA.** Hairworms *Gordius*
  Phylum **ANNELIDA.** Segmented worms
    Class *OLIGOCHAETA. Stylaria*
    Class *HIRUDINEA.* Leeches. *Haemopis*
  Phylum **BRYOZOA.** Moss animals *Plumatella*
  Phylum **MOLLUSCA**
    Class *GASTROPODA*. Water snails
    Class *BIVALVIA.* Mussels and cockles
  Phylum **ARTHROPODA.** Jointed-limbed animals
    Class *CRUSTACEA*
    Subclass *BRANCHIOPODA*
      Order Anostraca. Fairy shrimps *Chirocephalus*

Order NOTOSTRACA. Apus *Triops*
Order DIPLOSTRACA
  Sub-order CLADOCERA. *Daphnia*
SUBCLASS *OSTRACODA. Cypris*
SUBCLASS *COPEPODA. Cyclops*
SUBCLASS *BRANCHIURA.* Fish lice *Argulus*
Subclass *MALACOSTRACA*
  Suborder ISOPODA. Freshwater louse *Asellus*
  Suborder AMPHIPODA. Freshwater shrimps *Gammarus*
  Suborder DECAPODA. Crayfish *Austropotamobius*
Class *INSECTA*. Insects.
Subclass *APTERYGOTA*
  Order COLLEMBOLA. Water springtails
Subclass *PTERYGOTA*
EXOPTERYGOTA
  Order EPHEMEROPTERA. Mayflies
  Order ODONATA. Dragonflies
  Order PLECOPTERA. Stoneflies
  Order HEMIPTERA. Water bugs
ENDOPTERYGOTA
  Order MEGALOPTERA. Alderflies
  Order NEUROPTERA. Spongeflies and *Osmylus*
  Order TRICHOPTERA. Caddis flies
  Order LEPIDOPTERA. China mark moths
  Order COLEOPTERA. Beetles
  Order DIPTERA. Two-winged flies
  Order HYMENOPTERA. Ichneumon flies *Agriotypus*
Class *ARACHNIDA*
  Order ARANEA. Water spider
  Order ACARI. Water mites
Phylum **TARDIGRADA**. Water bears
Phylum **CHORDATA**. Vertebrates
Class *CYCLOSTOMATA*. Lampreys
Class *PISCES*. Fish
Class *AMPHIBIA*. Frogs, toads and newts

SINGLE-CELLED ANIMALS

The Protozoa are usually referred to as the single-celled animals, although perhaps non-cellular would be a better description, since all the functions of a living animal—moving about, ingesting food, excreting waste and reproduction—are undertaken by a single unit.

All Protozoa are microscopically small and since they display such a diversity of form and mode of life they have been accorded the status of a distinct sub-kingdom. Many kinds occur in freshwater and the principal groups are as follows:

Mastigophora (Flagellata)

The flagellates probably represent a border line between plants and animals. They are all very small, single-celled organisms and possess one or more whip-like swimming appendages called flagella which, however, are not always easy to observe under the microscope. Although some flagellates clearly have affinities with the animal kingdom since they feed on organic materials, others such as *Euglena* (**99**) are usually found to be feeding as plants, utilizing chlorophyll to effect photosynthesis. On the other hand some species of *Euglena* lose their chlorophyll if kept in the dark and yet survive, presumably by absorbing organic substances in the water.

Ceratium (**97**) is a common constituent of the plankton of lakes and other large stretches of water.

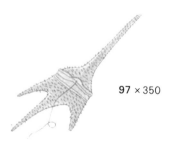

97 × 350

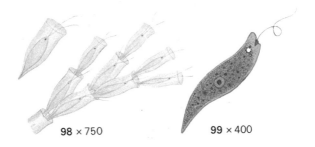

98 × 750   **99** × 400

Dinobryon (**98**) is another common constituent of the plankton of lakes.

Euglena (**99**) is abundant in small bodies of water particularly farmyard pools and others similarly rich in organic matter, when they may form a green scum on the surface of the water. At least 5 species are known.

Rhizopoda (Sarcodina)

This class includes the various species of *Amoeba* (**100**, **101**), the best known of all the Protozoa. Members of this order are merely unprotected blobs of protoplasm but in *Arcella* (**102**) and *Difflugia* (**104**) there are protective shells. The sun animal *Actinophrys sol* (**103**) has long ray-like pseudopodia, or 'false-feet' which capture prey and assist locomotion.

Amoeba (**100**, **101**) occurs most frequently on the mud surfaces or in the decaying matter on the bottom of ponds. If some of this material is left to stand in a tube of water, the amoebae, if present, will be visible after a few hours on the glass sides of the tube.

Actinophrys (**103**) is among water plants in ponds. *Actinosphaerium* is similar in appearance but ten times larger (up to 1 mm in diameter) and has a distinct annulus, or ring, all round the circumference of the body.

Difflugia (**104**) has a shell made of sand grains. Among the mud of ponds and sphagnum bogs.

Arcella (**102**) is found among plants or on the mud in ponds.

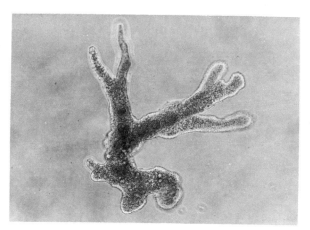

100 *Amoeba* × 100

101 × 100

102 × 350

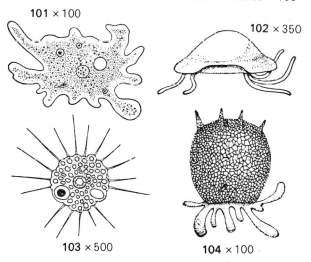

103 × 500

104 × 100

Sporozoa
The members of this class are parasites of other animals and frequently have complex life histories involving several hosts. *Glugea* attacks fish and produces characteristic whitish swellings on the hosts' body. *Lanchesterella* is a parasite of frogs and lives in their blood.

Ciliophora
The ciliates possess hair-like structures known as cilia which by their rhythmic waving propel the animal through the water or create currents to bring floating particles to them.

Several kinds appear when hay or other dried vegetation is allowed to stand in a jar of water for a few days in a warm place, such as an airing-cupboard. From their occurrence in such 'hay infusions' these organisms were formerly called 'infusorians'.

The slipper animal, *Paramecium* (**108**), is one of the commonest and the best known through being used as a biological 'type'.

Of the sessile kinds, the bell animals, *Vorticella* (**113**) and the branched forms *Campanella* (**116**) and *Carchesium* (**114**) are common and are found attached to plants or even to other animals. *Stentor* (**115**), although sometimes attached to plants, is frequently encountered swimming freely but then displays a rounder shape than that illustrated.

Colpidium (**105**) is a very common ciliate which is one of the first organisms to appear in hay infusions.

Loxodes (**106**) occurs in infusions which have been allowed to stand for some time.

Bursaria (**107**) is found most commonly in still pools, particularly where there are rotting beech leaves.

Paramecium (**108**) occurs naturally, though usually sparsely among decaying vegetation, but is easily cultured from hay infusions.

Coleps (**109**) is found among the decaying vegetation at the margins of still waters. It swims rapidly, turning over and over as it goes.

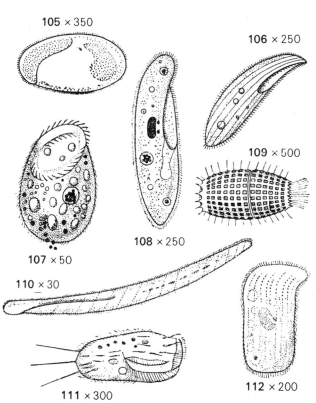

105 × 350

106 × 250

109 × 500

108 × 250

107 × 50

110 × 30

111 × 300

112 × 200

Spirostomum (**110**) is found in shallow pools often congregating in whitish masses on decaying leaves. It contracts to about a quarter its normal length when disturbed.

Stylonchia (**111**) is found among decaying vegetation and in old hay infusions.

Chilodon (**112**) is found among decaying vegetation in shady pools. It is often green in colour.

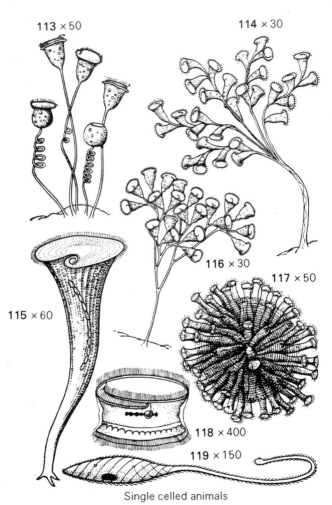

113 ×50

114 ×30

115 ×60

116 ×30

117 ×50

118 ×400

119 ×150

Single celled animals

Vorticella (**113**), bell animals, are very common in still water attached, often in large groups, to plants and freshwater crustacea.

Carchesium (**114**) is a colonial bell-animal, a number of individuals being attached to a common, much branched and *contractile* stalk. It occurs in ponds on dead sticks, etc.

Stentor (**115**) is found both free-swimming and attached to water plants in ponds.

Campanella (**116**) resembles *Carchesium* but the stalk is *non-contractile*, and the branches do not join directly to the main stem but terminate in V-shaped junctions. It is found in ponds on submerged vegetation and on crustaceans.

Ophrydium (**117**) is a colonial bell-animal forming a jelly-like mass attached to water plants or free floating in ponds and lakes.

Trichodina (**118**) is usually seen moving up and down the tentacles of *Hydra*.

Lacrymaria (**119**) is found in ponds. The 'neck' is contractile.

CELLULAR ANIMALS

The remaining animals described in this book belong to the sub-kingdom Metazoa, the cellular animals. In all their wide diversity they have in common the single fact that their body structure consists of many individual cells.

SPONGES

Two species of sponges live in freshwater—the river sponge *Ephydatia fluviatilis* (**127**) and the pond sponge *Spongilla lacustris* (**124**). The common names are, however, not to be taken too literally as indicating their usual habitats.

They are found as encrusting masses on stones, plants, submerged roots of trees, or on the sides of canals or river locks. Normally of a creamy-white colour, they may appear green through the presence of cells of the green alga *Chlorella*. When the colonies are large in late summer or autumn, the pond sponge tends to produce long finger-like outgrowths, whereas the river sponge is usually flatter. A certain identification is possible, however, by crushing a small piece of sponge and examining under 10 × objective of the microscope the flinty spicules which will be seen in the broken-down material. If these are as illustrated, with small rough-surfaced examples as well as the long smooth spicules, the species under examination is *Spongilla lacustris*. *Ephydatia fluviatilis* has only long smooth spicules.

In autumn the surface of sponges will be found studded with small spherical brown bodies. These are the gemmules: tough-walled resting stages which are released when the parent colony disintegrates in winter, and give rise to new sponges the following spring. A sexual form of reproduction also takes place in summer resulting in a ciliated larva which swims through the water before settling down to establish a new colony. The larvae of three species of sponge flies (126) live in the cavities of sponges.

Pond sponge, *Spongilla lacustris* (124) showing the characteristic finger-like growth of a mature colony.

Spicules of pond sponge (125). The presence of small 'woolly-bear' type of spicules among the larger plain ones, serves to identify the species of this sponge.

River sponge, *Ephydatia fluviatilis* (127), encrusting a stone.

HYDRAS

Four species of hydras are recognized in Britain. The green hydra, *Chlorohydra viridissima* (121), is easily distin-guished by its colour, derived from the presence of *Chlorella* in its body. The brown hydra, *Hydra oligactis* (123), usually has a slender portion or 'foot' at the base of the body column. The slender hydra. *H. attenuata* (122), has no 'foot'. *Cordylophora lacustris* (120) is a colonial hydra which has spread from brackish waters.

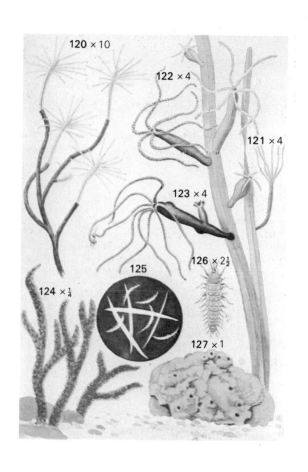

120 × 10

122 × 4

121 × 4

123 × 4

124 × ¼

125

126 × 2½

127 × 1

Sponges and hydras

Hydras are found on the stems and leaves of submerged plants but are easily overlooked since they contract into a very small compass when disturbed. The easiest way to find them is to draw a plankton net vigorously through a mass of water plants and then watch carefully for the hydras which have been dislodged falling down the glass tube attached to the net.

They catch small animals for food by means of harpoon-like structures called nematocytes, some of which sting and paralyse the prey while others secure it. When food is plentiful hydras develop buds which eventually break free but they also reproduce sexually.

Cordylophora lacustris (**120**) is a brackish water species which has now established itself in some river estuaries and on the Norfolk Broads.

Green hydra, *Chlorohydra viridissima* (**121**) is a very common species but one easily overlooked because of its colour resemblance to the plants to which it attaches itself. Body column when extended about 6 mm. Tentacles short and never as long as the body.

Slender hydra, *Hydra attenuata* = *H. vulgaris* (**122**) is the smallest species, the body column rarely exceeding 6 mm when extended, and having no 'stalk' at the base. Tentacles never more than two or three times the length of the body.

Brown hydra, *H. oligactis* (**123**), shown with a bud and reproductive bodies showing as swellings on the body tube, is recognized by the slender stalk or 'foot' at the base of the body column. Length of body column 12 mm or more and tentacles three or four times this length.

FLATWORMS

Of the flatworms that occur in freshwater, the observer is most likely to encounter the various species of planarians, which are found generally on the undersides of stones or leaves, but may sometimes be seen crawling rapidly on the bottom mud, or even on the underside of the surface film. They feed on small animals, fish eggs and the like.

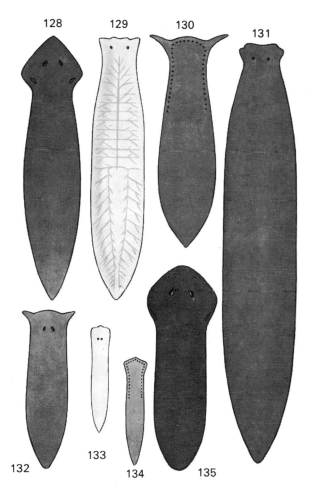

Planarian flatworms

Their eggs are laid in cocoons on stones or water plants.

Smaller but often with brilliant colouring are the *Rhabdocoeles* which are fairly common in ditches and other still waters in summer. *Dalyellia viridis* is sometimes green in colour. *Microstomum* is a parasite of *Hydra*, the stinging cells of which are absorbed, migrate to the skin, and become defence organs of the flatworm.

Other freshwater flatworms are parasitic on various animals and their life histories may include stages passed in several hosts.

Illustrated are eight of the eleven species of planarians occurring in Britain. (The actual sizes are indicated against each species.)

Dugesia tigrina (**128**) is an introduced American species, mottled grey and brown, single pair of eyes, mobile lateral tentacles. Size 25 mm.

Dendrocoelum lacteum (**129**) is common throughout the country, and easily recognized by its whitish colour and large size. Widely spaced single pair of eyes. Size 25 mm.

Polycelis felina (**130**) is found mainly in streams under stones. Distinguished by the long tentacles in conjunction with the large number of eyes. Size 20 mm.

Bdellocephala punctata (**131**) usually occurs on the under-surfaces of stones in lakes, and distinguished by its large size. A single pair of eyes. Size 39 mm.

Crenobia alpina (**132**) is found in small, cool streams, migrating to the cooler water upstream in summer and descending to lower levels in winter. Usually greyish in colour. Small but pronounced tentacles and single pair of eyes. Size 15 mm.

Phagocata vitta (**133**) is a small white worm with one pair of eyes close together. In cool streams, lakes, springs and caves. Size 10 mm.

Polycelis nigra (**134**) is distinguishable by large number of eyes (no tentacles). A very common species. Size 10 mm.

Dugesia lugubris (**135**) is black or dark brown in colour. Single pair of eyes have white patch round them which gives the doleful effect denoted by specific epithet *lugubris*. Size 19 mm.

ROTIFERS

These exquisite but microscopic animals are very abundant in freshwater and over 500 species occur in Britain. Most are free-swimming, others live attached to water plants, and some are parasitic. The characteristic crown of cilia, which from its resemblance in some species to the escapement wheel of a watch, has given rise to the name Rotifera (L. *rota* a wheel; *fero*, bear) creates currents in the water which bring food particles to the mouth and, in the free-swimming kinds, serves to propel the animals through the water. Nearly all rotifers that are found are females; male rotifers are small, degenerate creatures and throughout most of the season the development of eggs proceeds without fertilization by them. In spring and autumn, however, males appear and fertilize a special kind of 'resting-egg' which can withstand adverse conditions.

Limnias ceratophylli (**136**) is a common tube-dwelling rotifer. The case is made of a bodily secretion but it is frequently covered with adhering particles of material. The crown of cilia has only two lobes.

Conochilus hippocrepis (= *C. volvox*) (**137**) forms free-

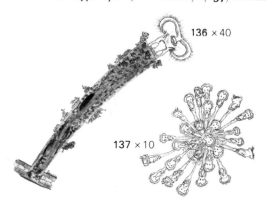

136 × 40

137 × 10

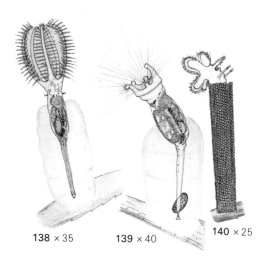

138 × 35   **139** × 40   **140** × 25

swimming colonies which roll through the water and are just visible to the naked eye. Common in lakes and clear ponds.

Stephanoceros fimbriatus (**138**) is a beautiful creature, somewhat local in its distribution, but when found it may occur in large numbers on water milfoil, Canadian pondweed and other plants.

Collotheca ornata (**139**) is another lovely creature, fairly common in clear ponds and lakes. The transparent sheath is not always easy to see.

Floscularia ringens (**140**) is common on the stems and leaves of water plants. The case is made of separate 'bricks' and the crown of cilia has four lobes.

Synchaeta pectinata (**141**) is an open-water rotifer of a characteristic cone-shape. The eye is unusual in being *blue*.

66

Philodina roseola (**142**) is one of the bdelloid or leech-like rotifers, so called because they move about rather like leeches. This species is frequently found in an encysted state in reddish sediment in dried-up rain gutters or bird-baths, sometimes in association with the alga *Haematococcus pluvialis*.

Keratella quadrata (**143**) is a common species in lakes and ponds.

Ascomorphella volvocicola (**144**) is a parasite of *Volvox*, living within the hollow sphere and feeding on the daughter cells.

Trichocerca rattus (**145**) is a common and widely distributed species in ponds.

Rotaria rotatoria (**146**) is one of the commonest rotifers and found among the weeds of ponds.

Brachionus calyciflorus (**147**) is a species of large rotifers with a characteristic urn-shaped shell, armed with spines. Identification of the species depends largely on the size

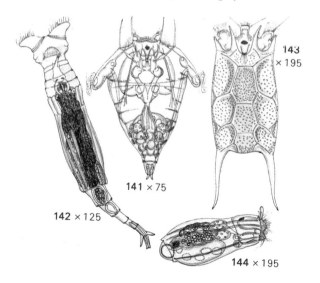

143
× 195

141 × 75

142 × 125

144 × 195

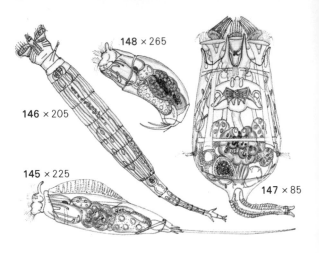

146 × 205

148 × 265

145 × 225

147 × 85

and form of the spines. *B. calyciflorus*, a common species in ponds and ditches, has four spines on the front of the shell and none behind.

Trichocerca porcellus (**148**) is found commonly in weedy ponds and ditches, often among filamentous algae.

ROUNDWORMS

These long, thread-like creatures are abundant in freshwater habitats (**149**), some being free-living whereas others are parasites of other animals. As they are extremely difficult to identify except by those who have specialized in their study, they are outside the scope of this little book.

Close relatives of the roundworms, however, are the hair-worms, Gordiodea (**151**), the adult stages of which are fairly common in ponds in spring and early summer. They resemble horse-hairs and are about 15 cm long. The larvae (**150**) are parasitic on various aquatic insects such as water beetles, dragonflies, and land insects including grasshoppers, etc.

68

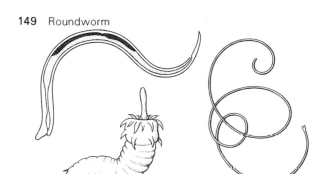

150 hairworm larva   **151** hairworm

ANNELID WORMS

Annelid worms have bodies formed of successive segments, all fairly similar to one another. Annelids are divided into three classes: Polychaeta with many bristles on the body and mostly marine; Oligochaeta, with few bristles; and Hirudinea with no bristles.

SEGMENTED WORMS

The illustrations show representatives of the commonest genera of freshwater oligochaetes. They are found generally in the mud of ponds, lakes and in some cases streams, where some make tubes or tunnels. Others are found in the stems or among the roots of water plants.

Family Lumbricidae

Eiseniella tetraedra (**153**) Pinkish in colour and resembling a small earthworm. Found in mud or among vegetation in still and running water. Size up to 50 mm.

Family Naididae

Chaetogaster (**155**) Colourless worms about 10 mm long. 5 species.

Nais (**154**) Colourless or pale pinkish. Found mainly in the mud waters where they make loosely constructed tubes. Size 15 mm. 8 species.

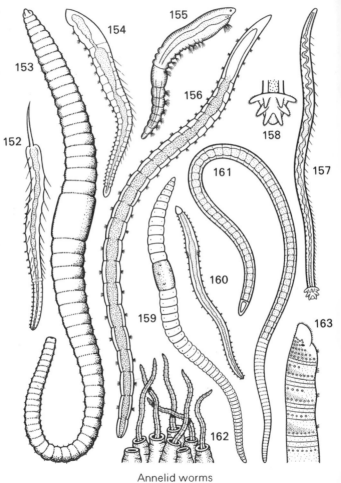

Annelid worms

70

Stylaria lacustris (**152**) Easily recognized by the long, narrow proboscis. Found among vegetation. Size 15 mm.

Dero (**157**) Six species. Pinkish in colour with a number of retractable gills (**158**) at the posterior end of the body. They live in mud tubes. Size 15 mm.

Ophidonais—head end (**163**) Live in mud. Size up to 75 mm. 2 species.

Family Tubificidae

Tubifex (**156**) Red worms living in mud with 'tail' end only protruding and waving about (**162**). Size 40 mm. 7 species.

Family Lumbriculidae

Lumbriculus variegatus (**161**) Lives in mud tubes. Colour greenish with red colour of blood showing through. Length up to 80 mm. 1 species.

Family Enchytraeidae

Lumbricillus (**159**) 4 species.

Enchytraeus (**160**) The members of these two genera are called pot worms. Their white colouring (and in the case of *Enchytraeus* the stiffness of the body) frequently causes them to be mistaken for the plant roots among which they live. Size 25 mm. 3 species.

LEECHES

Leeches are readily distinguished by the suckers at the end of the body—a small one at the head end and a larger one at the posterior end—with which they attach themselves to their prey or move about. Most leeches suck the body fluids of other animals, but only the medicinal leech is capable of piercing the human skin. The undersides of stones in ponds, streams and rivers are likely places to search for leeches. There are 15 aquatic species and one amphibious species, *Trocheta subviridis*, in Britain and the commonest are illustrated together with, in each case, a diagram of the head to illustrate the number and arrangement of the eyes, on which identification is largely based.

71

Leeches with a proboscis

Piscicola geometra (**164**) is found mainly in running water and the margins of lakes. A parasite of fish, usually attaching themselves to the fins and cloacal regions. Size 25 mm.

Hemiclepsis marginata (**165**) is another fish parasite but found in smaller bodies of still water than the preceding species. Size 17 mm.

Theromyzon tessulatum (= *Protoclepsis tessellata*) (**166**) is found in both still waters and slow streams. It is a parasite of water fowl and sucks blood from the wall of the nose or mouth. Size 25 mm.

Glossiphonia complanata (**167**) occurs mainly in streams but sometimes in still water. Rather a sluggish leech; when disturbed it contracts into a lump and drops off its support. Sucks the body fluids of water snails. Size 15 mm.

Glossiphonia heteroclita (**168**) is found mainly in still waters or the quieter reaches of rivers. Also a parasite of water snails. Size less than 15 mm.

Helobdella stagnalis (**169**) is very common in ponds and lakes. Feeds on insect larvae, snails and crustaceans. Size 10 mm.

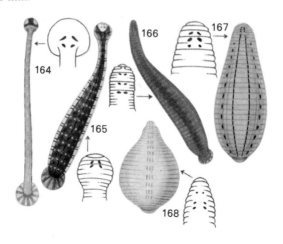

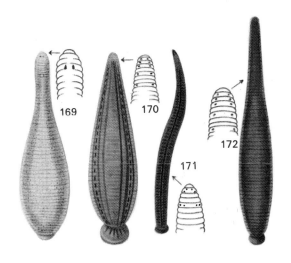

Leeches with jaws

Medicinal leech, *Hirudo medicinalis* (**170**), is rare, but occasionally found in ponds. It feeds on the blood of mammals, frogs, toads and fish. Size 90 mm.

Erpobdella (= *Herpodbella*) *octoculata* (**171**) is common in both running and still waters. Not a bloodsucker, but swallows whole insect larvae and crustaceans. The related *E. testacea* is found mainly in still waters. Size 40 mm.

Horse leech, *Haemopis sanguisuga* (**172**), is common in still waters and easily recognized by its large size. Not a bloodsucker but swallows worms, snails, etc. Size 60 mm.

MOSS ANIMALS (Bryozoa)

These are known also by the scientific name Polyzoa, derived from two Greek words meaning 'many animals' and refers to the mode of growth of these animals, many individuals being joined together so that they often resemble a patch of moss growing on stones or plants.

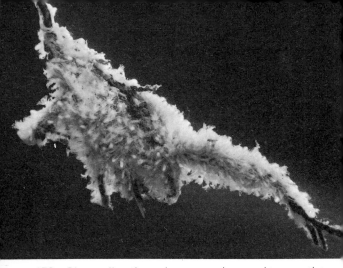

173 *Plumatella* × 1 ; a colony on a submerged tree rootlet

Most polyzoans live in the sea but a few occur in freshwater, usually where there are gentle currents or movement of the water, as in canals, boating lakes, etc. They are found attached to submerged wood, tree roots or water plant, but are easily overlooked, for when they are disturbed they retract and become mere jelly-like blobs. The tentacles bear cilia, the beating of which create currents in the water to bring food particles to the mouth. In late summer, tough walled seed-like objects, called statoblasts are formed internally and these are released when the parent colony disintegrates on the approach of winter, giving rise to new colonies in spring. The form of the statoblasts is characteristic of each species and thus useful for identification purposes.

Plumatella (**173**, **174**) is the commonest genus. The colonies, which may be of considerable size, are found attached to the underside of water-lily pads, tree rootlets and other submerged objects not exposed to full sunlight. 4 species. Statoblast (**175**).

74

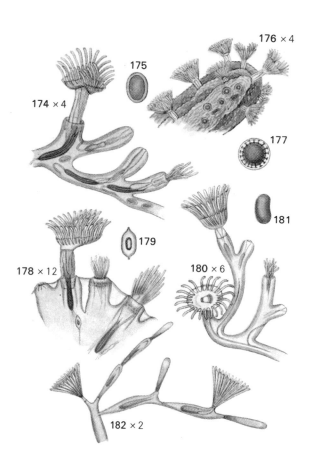

174 × 4

175

176 × 4

177

178 × 12

179

180 × 6

181

182 × 2

Moss animals

Cristatella mucedo (**176**) is found in colonies about 60 mm or more in length and somewhat resembling the egg mass of the pond snail *Lymnaea stagnalis*. It is found on water plants frequently in full sunlight. Statoblast (**177**).

Lophopus crystallinus (**178**) is larger individually than *Cristatella*, but colonies are smaller. It is found on stems of water plants. Statoblast (**179**).

Fredericella sultana (**180**), whose colonies are small and often covered with sand particles or algae, prefers shady places. Statoblast (**181**).

Paludicella articulata (**182**) colonizes by forming loose mossy bunches with characteristic branches of club-shaped cells joined end to end. No statoblasts have been observed in this species.

MOLLUSCS

Two classes of the large phylum MOLLUSCA are represented in fresh water: GASTROPODA, the snails and limpets, and BIVALVIA, the mussels and cockles. The most obvious difference between these two groups is the form of the shell. In Bivalvia it consists of two parts, or valves, hinged together—hence the term *Bivalves* applied to this class. In the Gastropoda, on the other hand, the shell is all in one piece and they are referred to as *Univalves*.

In both cases, within the shell lies the soft, unsegmented body, but it is important to remember that the shell is not merely an external shelter as is, for instance, the case of a caddis larva, but is an integral part of the mollusc and is attached to the body by powerful muscles.

The foot, a muscular development of the under surface of the body, is the structure with which both mussels and snails move about. In the mussels it is triangular in shape and can be protruded through the front end of the open shell, firstly to plough through the mud while the animal is on the move and then to anchor it when it has found a suitable place in which to settle.

In snails the foot forms a flat sole on which they glide along.

An important structure in all molluscs is the *mantle*, a fold of the body-wall which forms two lobes, one on each side of the body in bivalves and covering much of the body of univalves. The mantle secretes the materials of which the shell is made and since identification of molluscs depends mainly on the shape and structure of the shells, it may be well to say a few words about the formation of shell.

The principal constituent of the shell is calcium carbonate or 'chalk', but there are, in fact, three distinct layers in a mollusc shell. The outer layer which is thin and serves as a skin-like protection to the rest consists of *conchyolin*, a substance resembling the hard chitin of insects. This layer frequently gets rubbed off on parts of the shell subject to wear, and reveals the middle layer which provides the thickness of the shell, consisting mainly of calcium carbonate, with the crystals arranged perpendicularly to the surface. The inner lining of the shell, next to the animal's body, is the smooth mother-of-pearl or *nacre*, also consisting of calcium carbonate but with the crystals arranged parallel to the surface.

Nacre is secreted over the whole surface of the mantle, whereas the materials for the two outer layers of the shell are provided by the edges of the mantle and thus the shell is extended at its edges as the mollusc grows.

Throughout the season there are periods of rapid growth alternating with periods of slower development so that the shell does not increase in size uniformly, and lines of growth, parallel to the edges, often indicate the age of the specimen. A changing environment, too, will frequently result in differences in the outer regions of the shell.

The shell of a snail (**183**) is really a long conical tube twisted into a series of coils, each of which is called a *whorl*. The first whorl, at the apex of the shell in the case of a pond-snail, is the part originally occupied by the newly hatched snail and the rest of the whorls are added

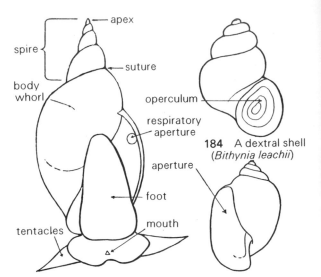

183 Great pond snail (*Lymnaea stagnalis*) showing parts **185** A sinistral shell (*Physa acuta*)

one by one, as the snail grows. The largest whorl is called the body-whorl and the rest, collectively comprise the *spire*. Divisions between the whorls are termed *sutures*.

On holding a pointed shell so that its apex is upwards, the opening will usually be found to be on the observer's right-hand side. Such a shell is said to be *dextral* (**184**). If, however, the opening is to the left, it is said to be *sinistral* (**185**). Most species of snails are dextral, although sinistral coiling is characteristic of a few, but individuals are sometimes encountered which do not conform to the rule for their species and may cause difficulties in identification for the uninitiated.

Since calcium carbonate enters so largely into the constitution of the shell, waters seriously deficient in calcium—'soft' waters—will not provide conditions suitable for molluscs and these animals will be absent or

186 Great pond snail

represented only by stunted specimens. Individual species vary in their ability to tolerate calcium deficiencies and the wandering snail, *Lymnaea pereger* (**189**), for instance, can apparently thrive in quite soft waters, in contrast to the great pond snail, *L. stagnalis* (**186**, **195**), which is essentially a hard-water species.

It is perhaps worth remembering that hard waters generally have more plant growth than soft waters, and thus by providing more food and shelter, offer better conditions for molluscs on these grounds alone.

WATER-SNAILS AND FRESHWATER LIMPETS

These comprise the freshwater gastropods, and belong to two subclasses, Prosobranchia and Pulmonata.

The prosobranchians, or gill-breathers, are molluscs with a horny or chalky plate, the operculum, attached to the foot, with which they can close their shell; they are thus called the operculates as well. They breathe by means of gills.

The pulmonates on the other hand are molluscs without

an operculum, able to breathe atmospheric air by means of a 'lung'.

The prosobranchians are truly aquatic creatures and still retain the method of respiration of their marine ancestors—by gills. The freshwater pulmonates on the other hand are terrestrial snails that have taken to an aquatic life, and they still come to the surface to take in atmospheric air by means of a lung. When the supply of dissolved air in the water is good, however, as it is in most ponds in cold weather, even these snails can apparently obtain sufficient oxygen for their needs from the water.

The freshwater prosobranchians live mainly in well-oxygenated and clear waters, particularly in rivers and streams. They include the freshwater winkles, Genus: *Viviparus* (**187**, **196**); the valve snails, *Valvata* (**193**); the nerite, *Theodoxus fluviatilis* (**204**); Jenkins' spire shell, *Potamophyrgus jenkinsi* (**190**) and two species of *Bithynia* (**191**). Most of them have separate sexes but Jenkins' spire shell is parthenogenetic; that is reproducing without a male sex. This snail and the freshwater winkles do not lay eggs but give birth to living young.

187 Freshwater winkles

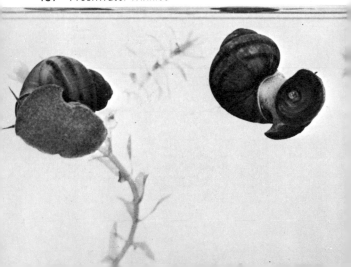

The pulmonates are all *hermaphrodite*, that is each snail has both male and female parts, and all are capable of laying eggs. Although self-fertilization can take place in some species, the more usual method of reproduction is by the union of two individuals.

The eggs in their jelly capsules are familiar objects on submerged stones and plants, and the number of eggs in each cluster varies within wide limits even in individuals of the same species. It has been noticed that these eggs are sometimes carried on the feet of waterbirds and in this way snails are introduced to waters miles away from their original source.

Included among the pulmonates are the familiar pond snails of the genus *Lymnaea*; the ramshorn snails, *Planorbis* etc. (**197–202**); the bladder snails, *Physa* (**207**), and the freshwater limpets (**203**).

The last-named molluscs, of which two species are found in Britain, the lake limpet *Acroloxus lacustris* (**203**) and the larger river limpet *Ancylus fluviatilis* have shells of a different type from the other water-snails. They are hood shaped, with no whorls, and the edges, consisting only of the soft, horny outer layers of shell, are able to adhere firmly to surfaces which may be rough.

The food of water-snails consists mainly of algae attached to water-plants or stones. Decaying parts of higher plants may be eaten, but rarely are the healthy parts attacked. The great pond snail (**186, 195**) occasionally takes animal food, dead or alive.

Of the 52 species of water-snails found in Britain, 14 of these are prosobranchians.

Prosobranchians

Jenkins' spire shell, *Potamopyrgus jenkinsi* (**190**), is now common in running water habitats but before 1893 it was purely a brackish water species. Size 5 mm.

Common bithynia *Bithynia tentaculata* (**191**), is common in larger bodies of still water and streams. *B. leachii*, a smaller and less common species is found mainly in the south and east of England. Size 11 mm.

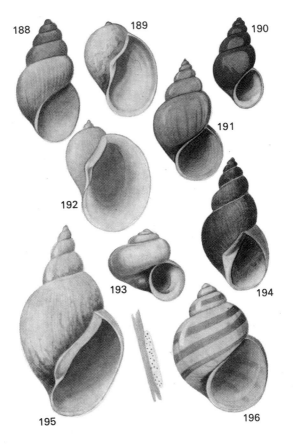

Freshwater snails

Valve snail, *Valvata piscinalis* (**193**), is common in rivers and streams with a gentle flow. The valve snails are easily recognized by the snout-like appendage on the head between the tentacles. Size 6 mm.

Freshwater winkle, *Viviparus viviparus* (**187, 196**), is fairly common in running water in the south and midland parts of England and in Wales. Size 3·5 mm.

Nerite, *Theodoxus fluviatilis* (**204**), occurs in the swifter regions of calcareous rivers attached to stones or plants. Size 6 mm.

Pulmonates

Dwarf pond snail, *Lymnaea truncatula* (**188**), is common at the edges of small streams and ditches and in swampy pastures. An intermediate host of the liverfluke of sheep. Size 9 mm.

Wandering snail, *L. pereger* (**189**), is the commonest mollusc and found everywhere, even in brackish water. The shell is very variable in form. Size 12 mm.

Ear pond snail, *L. auricularia* (**192**), is fairly common in calcareous waters. Size 13 mm.

Marsh snail. *L. palustris* (**194**), is found mainly in marshes and ditches, although it does occur also in lakes and rivers. Size 22 mm.

Great pond snail, *L. stagnalis* (**186, 195**), is a species which favours large ponds rich in calcium, but is also found in slowly flowing rivers and canals. Size 5 cm.

Keeled ramshorn, *Planorbis carinatus* (**197**), is common in larger bodies of calcareous water. Size 15 mm.

Whirpool ramshorn, *P. vortex* (**198**), is common in calcareous waters; usually in rivers and streams but sometimes in ponds. Size 9 mm.

Ramshorn, *P. planorbis* (**199**) is common. Size 12 mm.

Flat ramshorn *Segmentina complanata* (**200**), is common in ponds. Size 4·5 mm.

White ramshorn, *P. albus* (**201**), is easily recognized by the dull white colour of the shell. It is common in ponds, lakes and streams. Size 7 mm.

Button ramshorn, *P. leucostoma* (**202**), is common in marshy places, although also found in lakes. Size 7·5 mm.

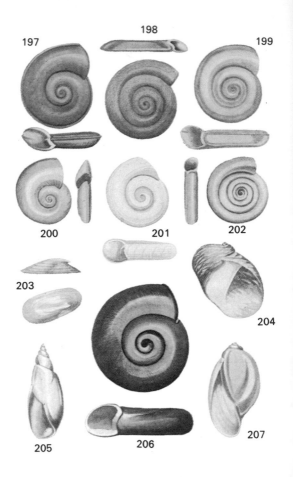

Freshwater snails

208 Great ramshorn snail

Lake limpet, *Acroloxus lacustris* (**203**), is common in still waters, usually attached to water plants. The larger river limpet, *Ancylus fluviatilis*, is a common species found mainly in flowing water or at the edges of lakes. Size 4·5 mm.

Moss bladder snail, *Aplexa hypnorum* (**205**), is fairly common in ditches and ponds. Size 10 mm.

Great ramshorn, *Planorbarius corneus* (**206**, **208**), is fairly common in larger bodies of calcareous water. Size 28 mm.

Bladder snail, *Physa fontinalis* (**207**), is common in clear streams and lakes. Size 10 mm.

MUSSELS AND COCKLES

These, the bivalves, include the mussels, the smaller orb-shell and pea-shell cockles, and the zebra mussel—a total of twenty-seven species.

Larger mussels   All the larger mussels belong to the super-family Unionacea. They live at the bottom of the water with part of the shell sunk into the mud and the two valves held slightly apart. Two tubes, or siphons, are

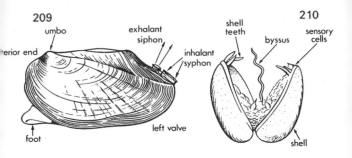

209

umbo

exhalant siphon

inhalant syphon

anterior end

foot

left valve

210

shell teeth

byssus

sensory cells

shell

protruded from the rear end of the shell, the upper one being the exhalant siphon, and the lower fringed one, the inhalant siphon. Through these a continuous current of water is drawn through the mantle cavity and then expelled, bringing a supply of both oxygen and food particles and eliminating waste materials (**209**).

There are distinct sexes, and the females during the summer produce large numbers of eggs which are passed to brood-pouches in the outer gills where they are fertilized by sperm from a nearby male taken in through the inhalant siphon. The larvae, called *glochidia* (**210**), are expelled during the following spring through the exhalant siphon and at first swim through the water by opening and closing their shells, but eventually many of them adhere to water plants by means of a coiled, sticky thread, the *byssus* which they possess. Their survival depends on becoming attached to a passing fish (often a stickleback) and those that are successful embed themselves into the skin of the fish and live a parasitic existence for about three months. At the end of that time they are fully developed and, dropping off their hosts, they settle down to lead a free existence. The larger mussels attain an age of about ten to fifteen years.

Painter's mussel, *Unio pictorum* (**211**), is found in rivers, canals, lakes and large ponds throughout England and Wales. The names, both common and scientific, were

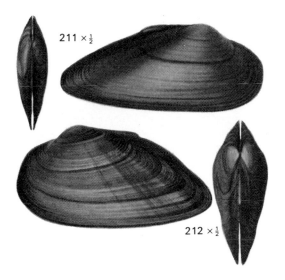

211 ×½

212 ×½

given because the valves of the shells were used by the early Dutch painters to hold their colours.

On the Continent this species is used by the fish, the bitterling, *Rhodeus sericeus*, as an incubator for its eggs. The female bitterling, by means of a long ovipositor, deposits her eggs into the mantle cavity of the mussel where they develop.

Unio tumidus (**212**), the shell of which is not so elongated as the previous species and is usually thicker, is not so common as the painter's mussel and is only found in clear rivers and canals from Yorkshire to Somerset and in parts of Wales.

Pearl mussel, *Margaritifera margaritifera* (**213**), is a dark, almost black species, found in swift rivers in the north of England, along the west coasts and in Scotland and Ireland. Pearls of commercial value are sometimes found in the shell and there was at one time a thriving pearl fishery on the River Tay in Perthshire. Other native

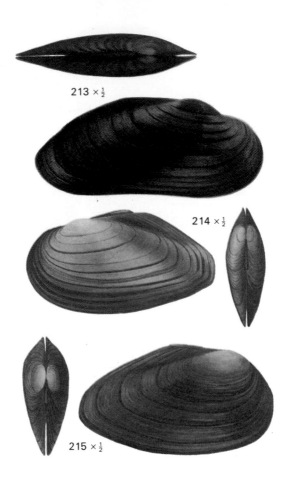

213 $\times \frac{1}{2}$

214 $\times \frac{1}{2}$

215 $\times \frac{1}{2}$

Freshwater mussels

freshwater mussels sometimes produce pearls but not in sufficient quantities to be commercially important. The pearls, which may be white, pink, green or brown, are produced in the same way as those of marine molluscs, by the excretion of nacre from the mantle to embed an irritant foreign body, such as an encysted parasitic worm.

Swan mussel, *Anodonta cygnea* (**214**), lives in large ponds, lakes, canals and rivers where there is a muddy bottom. Specimens up to 22 cm long have been recorded.

Duck mussel, *Anodonta anatina* (**215**), prefers running water with a sandy bottom and is well distributed in Britain. As both this and the last species are very variable it is not always easy to differentiate between them, but in general the shell of the duck mussel is smaller, more oval, thicker and darker in colour.

Orb-shell and Pea-shell Cockles   There are 4 species of orb-shells, *Sphaerium,* and 16 species of pea-shells, *Pisidium.* These are much smaller than the mussels, the shell of the largest species *Sphaerium rivicola* being about 27mm in length; some of the pea-shells are extremely small.

The orb-shells are distinguishable by having two siphons, the pea-shells possessing only one. This feature, of course, can only be seen in a living specimen which has opened its shell. The shells themselves however, are distinctive: usually those of orb-shells being more symmetrical and rounder, whereas those of the pea-shells look somewhat lopsided and flatter.

Both kinds of cockle are hermaphrodite and produce fully developed young—about six at a time, which do not go through a parasitic stage.

Horny orb-shell, *Sphaerium corneum* (**216**), is common in ponds and in streams throughout Britain even in soft waters, and is one of the larger members of this genus.

River pea-shell, *Pisidium amnicum* (**217**), is common and widely distributed in running water.

The distinctions between a typical orb-shell and a

216   217

typical pea-shell are clearly seen in these two illustrations: the more spherical and symmetrical shell and two siphons of orb-shells: the asymmetrical and flatter shell and single siphon of *Pisidium*.

Zebra mussel   This is a somewhat aberrant species bearing a closer resemblance to marine bivalves than to the freshwater forms, but is found in slow-rivers, docks and also in water-mains. It is believed to have been imported to this country about 1824 in timber ships from the Baltic. The length of the shell—from 35 to 50mm—and its characteristic markings of wavy bands of brown, serve to distinguish it from any other native bivalve. It produces a type of larva, called a *veliger*, which swims freely in the water by means of cilia, but eventually drops to the bottom, grows a shell and attaches itself to some solid support. Frequently groups of these molluscs are found growing together on submerged posts or stones.

Zebra mussel, *Dreissena polymorpha* (**218**), has very distinctive patterning on the shell which readily identifies this species. It is found attached to submerged objects in rivers, canals, docks, as well as in reservoirs and water-mains in England and parts of Wales.

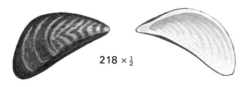

218 × ½

JOINTED-LIMBED ANIMALS

The great phylum of arthropods is well represented in freshwater and its members are estimated to comprise about three-quarters of the total creatures living there. Apart from the jointed limbs, specialized and adapted for particular purposes, arthropods are characterized by a hard shell, which serves as an external skeleton. The following groups of arthropods occur in freshwater:

CRUSTACEANS

Branchiopods

The branchiopods, or 'gill-footed' crustaceans include the fairy-shrimps and the water fleas (cladocerans). There are a great number both of species and individuals of water fleas and their role of converting the minute plant life into food for the larger animals makes them of immense importance in the economy of freshwater.

Simocephalus vetulus (**219**) is a very common species throughout the country. Usually among water plants. Size 3 mm.

Daphnia hyalina (**220**) is a transparent species found in open water. Size 2·5 mm.

Daphnia magna (**226**) is rarer, yellowish to reddish, found in warmer waters; female 3 to 5 mm; male 2 mm.

Sida crystallina (**221**) is common in most parts of the country among vegetation in ponds and lakes. It can adhere to objects by means of a gland at the back of the head. Size 3 mm.

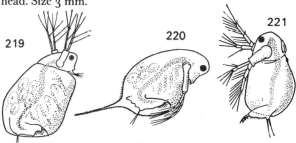

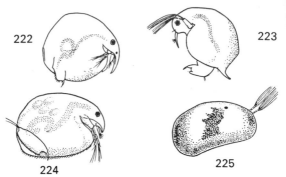

222

223

224

225

Chydorus ovalis (**222**) is a widely distributed species but very small. Swims less jerkily than the larger species. Size 0·5 mm.

Bosmina coregoni (**223**) is widely distributed in the north and midlands in open water zone of ponds and lakes. Size 1 mm.

Eurycercus lamellatus (**224**) is our largest cladoceran. Common throughout the country among weeds. This species seems liable to be trapped in the surface film. Size 4 mm.

Ostracods

The ostracods are all small creatures and have bean-shaped bivalve shells. They feed mainly on decaying organic material. *Cypris* (**225**) is a typical member of this sub-class, common in weedy ponds. Size about 1 mm. 2 species.

Copepods

The members of this subclass, which include the well-known *Cyclops* (**229**), are mainly pear-shaped and it is usually the females that are noticed as they carry their eggs with them in little sacs. Nauplius larva (**230**).

Canthocampus staphylinus (**227**) is common in ponds in the winter months when the females carry their single egg-sac. Size about 0·5 mm.

Diaptomus castor (**228**) is recognizable by the very long

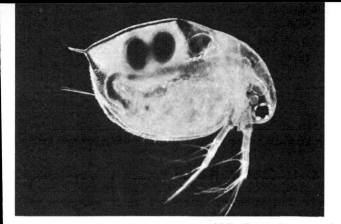

226 *Daphnia magna*

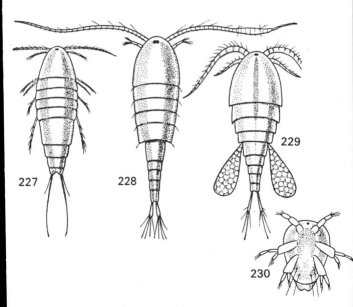

227

228

229

230

93

antennae. Common in ponds during the winter. (The closely related species *D. gracilis* and *D. vulgaris* occur also in summer.) Size about 2 mm.

Cyclops (**229**) is widely distributed throughout the country. Forepart of the body of *Cyclops* is broader than *Diaptomus*. Size about 2 mm. 5 species.

Fish lice

The fish lice are well adapted by the flatness of their bodies and their large suckers for holding on to the outside of their hosts. *Argulus* (**240**) is the only genus in freshwater.

Larger crustaceans

This subclass includes the relatively larger crustacea such as the water lice, *Asellus* (**231**), and freshwater shrimps, *Gammarus* (**235**). They are mainly scavengers, feeding on decaying plant and animal remains at the bottom of the water. It also includes the freshwater crayfish, *Austropotamobius pallipes* (**234**), which occurs in streams particularly in limestone districts.

Water Louse, *Asellus aquaticus* (**231, 232**), is a very common animal on the bottom and among the weeds of ponds and slow-moving streams. Size 20 mm.

Proasellus meridianus (**233**). The difference in pigmentation between *A. aquaticus* and the rarer species *Proasellus meridianus* is shown in these two figures.

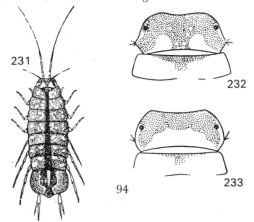

94

234 Freshwater crayfish

Apus, *Triops cancriformis* (**236**), is a rare crustacean found in pools which dry up in summer. Recorded from Kent, Hampshire, Gloucestershire and Kirkcudbrightshire. Size 20 mm.

Freshwater Shrimp, *Gammarus* (**235**). Three species of *Gammarus* occur in freshwater in Britain and others are found in brackish waters. Size 30 mm. T—telson.

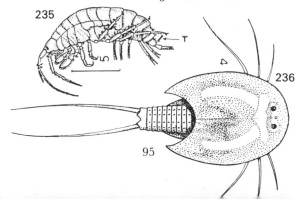

235

236

237 *Crangonyx pseudogracilis*

238 Nauplius larva of fairy shrimp

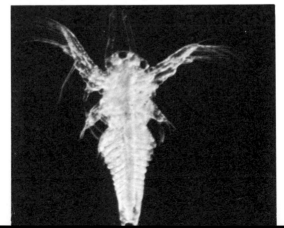

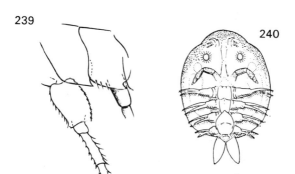

Crangonyx pseudogracilis (**237**) is an introduced species closely resembling *Gammarus* and now recorded from various parts of Britain. It can be distinguished by its smaller size, the serrations on the basal segments of legs 3 to 5 (**239**), and its habit of crawling in an upright position in contrast to *Gammarus* which crawls on its side. Size 20 mm.

Fish Louse, *Argulus foliaceus* (**240**), is a parasite of freshwater fish, attaching itself to almost any part of the exterior of the host. Size 7 mm.

Fairy Shrimp, *Chirocephalus diaphanus* (**241**), is another crustacean found in temporary pools. Size 25 mm. Nauplius larva (**238**).

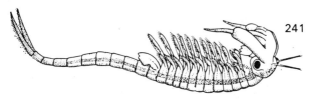

CLASSIFICATION OF AQUATIC INSECTS

Subclass	Division	Order
APTERYGOTA. wingless insects without metamorphosis		COLLEMBOLA, springtails (A few spp. live on surface film)
PTERYGOTA insects with one or two pairs of wings and undergoing metamorphosis	*Exopterygota*: wings develop externally, metamorphosis gradual or incomplete	EPHEMEROPTERA, mayflies ODONATA, damselflies and dragonflies PLECOPTERA, stoneflies HEMIPTERA, bugs
	Endopterygota: wings develop internally, metamorphosis complete (egg, larva, pupa, imago)	MEGALOPTERA, alderflies NEUROPTERA, spongeflies and *Osmylus* LEPIDOPTERA, moths and butterflies TRICHOPTERA, caddis flies DIPTERA, two-winged flies HYMENOPTERA, ichneumon flies etc. COLEOPTERA, beetles

Representatives of the twelve orders shown in the table on page 98 have adopted a life in or on fresh water; some live there only in their immature stages, whereas others, as for example the water beetles and water bugs, are aquatic also in their adult form.

Mayflies

The adult life of a mayfly is very short but the nymphal stage, which is entirely aquatic, may last one, two or even three years in some species. The transformation to a winged stage may take place at the surface of the water or on some waterside object depending on the species, but the creature which emerges is a sub-imago, with dull colouring and cloudy wings—the 'dun' of the fly-fisherman. The final moult to the fully adult insect—the 'spinner'—takes place shortly afterwards, and then follows the swarming of the males over the water so characteristic of this group of insects. When a female appears, part of the swarm follows her, often to a considerable height, where pairing takes place. The eggs are usually dropped into the water as the female flies over, although in some species she deposits them on submerged objects.

The nymphs feed mainly on plant material although some are believed to be partly carnivorous. In Britain 47 species occur. Based on their modes of life the nymphs can be grouped as follows and examples of each are illustrated: swimming nymphs (**243, 244, 247**); crawling nymphs (**245**); nymphs flattened for clinging to stones in fast-flowing water (**246, 248**); and burrowing nymphs (**249**).

Mayfly, or greendrake, *Ephemera danica* (**242**), is the adult insect, which emerges during the latter part of May or early June.

Mayfly nymphs

Pale watery dun, *Centroptilum luteolum* (**243**), is widely distributed among the weeds in rivers and lakes.

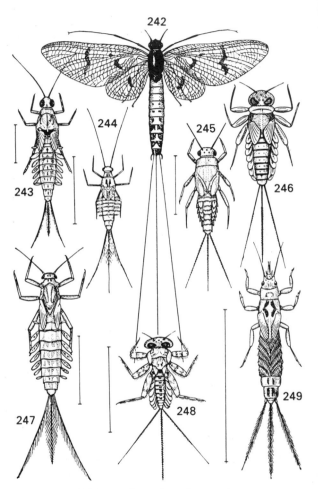

Adult mayfly and mayfly nymphs

Pond olive, *Cloeon dipterum* (**244**), is found in still waters including small ponds throughout Britain. It is very common.

Blue-winged olive, *Ephemerella ignita* (**245**), it is found on stones and vegetation in fast-moving waters. It is widely distributed.

Olive upright. *Rhithrogena semicolorata* (**246**), is very common in stony streams. *R. haarupi*, a less widely distributed species, is the 'March brown' of the angler.

Large dark olive. *Baetis rhodani* (**247**), is common and widely distributed in fast-moving waters.

Late March brown, *Ecdyonurus venosus* (**248**), is common and widely distributed in fast streams, clinging to the underside of stones. *E. dispar* is found also in lakes.

Mayfly or greendrake, *Ephemera vulgata* (**249**), is found in slow rivers in the south and midlands where it burrows in the mud. *E. danica* is more widely distributed, in lakes and rivers with a sandy bottom.

Damselflies and dragonflies

The damselflies and dragonflies attract even the casual observer by their brilliant colourings, their glistening wings and the strong purposeful flight of the larger kinds. There are 44 species in Britain and they are classified into two suborders, the members of which are easily distinguished:

ZYGOPTERA, the damselflies with slender bodies; two pairs of similar wings which are held vertically over the abdomen when at rest; fluttering flight. 17 species.

ANISOPTERA, the true dragonflies with two pairs of dissimilar wings, which are held out horizontally at right angles to the body when at rest; stouter bodies, strong flight. 27 species.

Both damselflies and dragonflies are carnivorous, capturing and devouring other insects, and even on occasions their own kind. The larger species have regular beats and fly backwards and forwards hunting for their prey. The beats are often some considerable distance from water. The damselflies on the other hand remain among the waterside vegetation.

The mating of these insects is effected in a curious way. The genitals of the male are in the last but one segment of the body. Sperm is transferred from there to special pairing organs on his second segment. The female is grasped at the back of the head by special anal (tail) claspers and in this position the pair fly in tandem to a suitable place, depending on the species, when the female bends back her body until her tail-end comes into contact with the pairing organs on the male's second segment, and fertilization takes place.

The eggs of some species are dropped into the water but in other species the female enters the water partly or completely to deposit them on submerged plants or other objects.

Damselflies

Green lestes, *Lestes sponsa* (**250–1**), is widely distributed and in some localities common, particularly in the south. It is the most likely small metallic green species to be observed as the only other one, *L. dryas* is very rare. It is seen flying feebly among waterside vegetation, rarely venturing over the open water. It is on the wing from July to September.

Large red damselfly, *Pyrrhosoma nymphula* (**252–3**), is our commonest red damsel fly and widely distributed throughout the country. It frequents still waters, including brackish pools. It is often the first dragonfly to be seen in the season and it remains on the wing from the beginning of May to the end of August.

Common ischnura, *Ischnura elegans* (**254–5**) is probably our commonest damselfly, particularly in south and eastern England. It is found in both still and gently flowing waters and is on the wing from the end of May to the end of August.

Common coenagrion, *Coenagrion puella* (= *Agrion puella*) (**256–7**), is widely distributed and common in England and Wales, but scarce in Scotland. One of the two

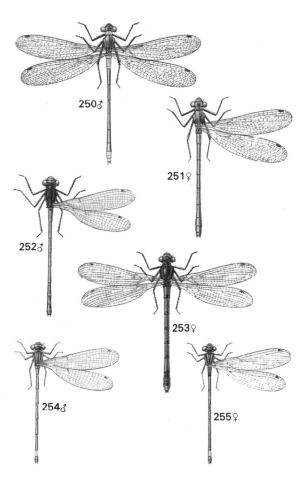

250♂

251♀

252♂

253♀

254♂

255♀

Damselflies (natural size)

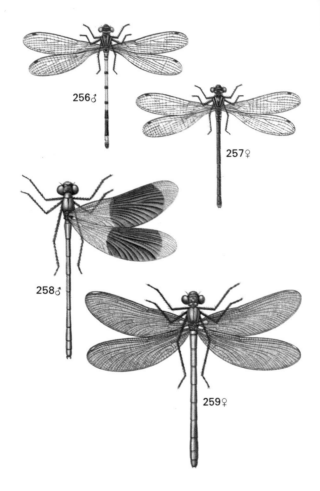

256♂

257♀

258♂

259♀

Damselflies (natural size)

common blue damselflies, being distinguished from *Enallagma cyathigerum* (**260–1**) by the larger amount of black on the thorax. Although usually found fluttering over or around still water habitats, it occasionally strays over adjoining fields. It is on the wing from the end of May to the middle of August.

Banded agrion, *Agrion splendens* (**258–9**), is a common damselfly in southern and midland England and Wales but scarce elsewhere. The broad, dark bands across the wings of the males and the greenish colouring of the wings of the females distinguish this species. It favours slow rivers, canals and lakes where there is a muddy bottom, and may be seen from the end of May to the end of August.

Common blue damselfly, *Enallagma cyathigerum* (**260–1**), is widely distributed and very common throughout Britain, favouring large stretches of water on heaths and commons and frequently on salt-marshes, in the brackish waters of which it may breed. It is on the wing from mid-May to mid-September.

Demoiselle agrion, *Agrion virgo* (**262–3**), is widely

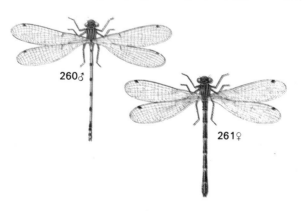

260♂

261♀

Damselflies (natural size)

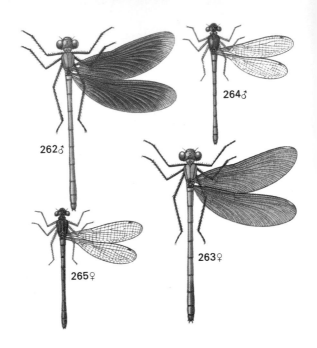

Damselflies (natural size)

distributed throughout Britain but commoner in the south. Although adult males are easily distinguishable from *A. splendens*, the females and young specimens are easy to confuse when they are flying. The species occurs near rivers, canals, lakes and ponds, particularly where they are shaded by trees, and is on the wing from the end of May to the end of August.

Small red damselfly, *Ceriagrion tenellum* (= *Pyrrhosoma tenellum*) (**264–5**), is restricted to the southern counties, in some of which it is locally abundant. It favours boggy or marshy pools, among the vegetation of which it flies feebly from early June to early September.

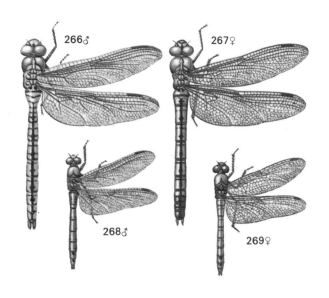

Dragonflies (¾ natural size)

Dragonflies

Emperor dragonfly, *Anax imperator* (**266–7**), is mainly a southern species and fairly common in the south east of Britain. It is one of our largest and handsomest species frequenting large stretches of water where among the surrounding vegetation it hawks for its prey, which include other dragonflies. It is on the wing from early June to early September.

Common sympetrum, *Sympetrum striolatum* (**268–9**), is common and widely distributed throughout Britain. It darts about in search of prey in a restless manner, although at times it may be seen resting on exposed places. On the wing from early July to as late as October.

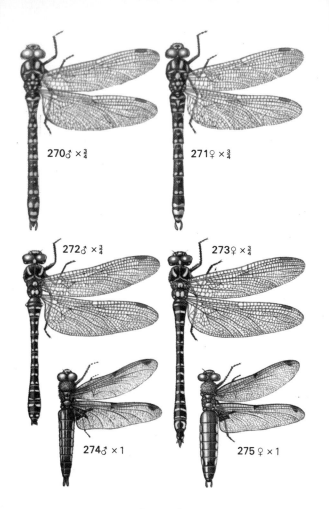

270♂ × ¾

271♀ × ¾

272♂ × ¾

273♀ × ¾

274♂ × 1

275♀ × 1

Dragonflies

Southern aeshna, *Aeshna cyanea* (**270–1**), is common in most southern and midland counties of England and Yorkshire but rare elsewhere. It searches for its prey chiefly around still water habitats, occasionally, however, patrolling a beat away from the water. Flies from early June to early September.

Golden-ringed dragonfly, *Cordulegaster boltonii* (**272–3**), is a large dragonfly, easily distinguished by the pronounced black and yellow banding all along the abdomen. It is plentiful in some areas, particularly in the west, but is not a common species. On the wing, usually over or near water, from mid-June to early September.

Four-spotted libellula, *Libellula quadrimaculata* (**274–5**), is common throughout the British Isles and easily recognized by the blotches of colour on the wings. Both sexes are alike in colouring. It may stray far from water in search of prey and often operates from a favourite perch, repeatedly leaving it to capture some insect and then returning. It is seen from the end of May to the end of August.

Common aeshna, *Aeshna juncea* (**276–7**), is common and

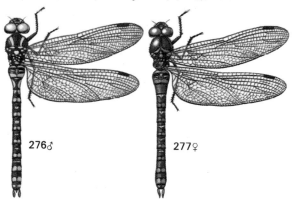

276♂   277♀

Dragonflies (¾ natural size)

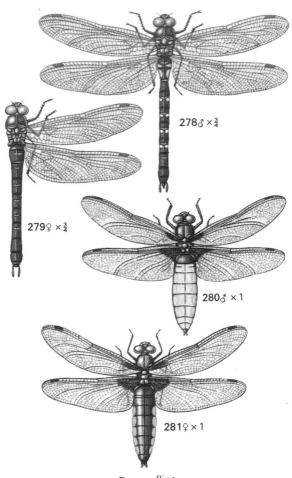

278♂ × ¾

279♀ × ¾

280♂ × 1

281♀ × 1

Dragonflies

110

widely distributed throughout Britain. It is distinguishable from the southern aeshna by its bluer colour. Its hawking beats are often far away from water, in woods or over moors, and it flies from mid-July to the end of September or later.

Brown aeshna, *A. grandis* (**278–9**), is very common in south and midland England but rarer farther north. It is one of our largest species and in flight, its yellow wings attract attention. It hawks for food well away from water, on occasions even coming into gardens. It is to be seen on the wing from mid-July to the end of September.

Broad-bodied libellula, *Libellula depressa* (**280–1**), is very common in the south and fairly common in the midlands, but absent as a breeding species in the north of England and Scotland. It sometimes breeds in brackish water on marshes and may be seen flying about in search of prey in such places. It is on the wing from the end of May to mid-August.

Nymphs of damselflies and dragonflies

The immature stage of these insects is entirely aquatic. In the damselflies it occupies a year but in dragonflies it may last two or three years. There are considerable differences in the nymphs of the two groups. Zygopterid nymphs are slender-bodied and possess three leaf-like gills at the tail end of the body. They vary in colouring from bright green to dull brown. Anisopterid nymphs are plump-bodied, lack the three 'tails,' and are drab-coloured. Some kinds, e.g. *Libellula,* are quite short, whereas others, such as *Aeshna,* are long-bodied. A 'mask,' a hinged structure formed from the fused third pair of jaws, or labrum, and bearing strong claws at its end, is common to both types of nymph. When not in use the mask is folded back under the head, and when prey is within reach it is shot out at great speed and the victim secured by the claws.

The nymphs are not normally active creatures although when alarmed, anisopterids can move quickly through the water, propelled by a jet of water ejected from the rectal cavity. In general, however, they remain quietly

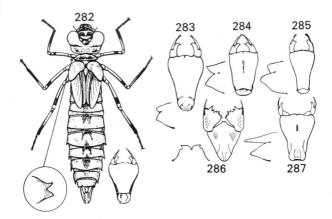

among water plants waiting for their prey, in the form of tadpoles, aquatic insects and crustaceans, to come within reach. They undergo about twelve moults of skin and at about the sixth, wing-buds become apparent on the back, and increase in size with each successive moult.

Emergence takes place from May until August, depending on the species and weather conditions, the nymph climbing out of the water up the stem of a water plant. The nymphal skin splits down the back of the thorax and this releases the head, thorax and legs of the imago. After a rest, the abdomen is extricated and finally the wings expand through the pressure of body fluid in them. A short period then elapses before the body hardens and the insect flies away in search of food or a mate. The adults may live a month or so but do not survive the winter.

Dragonfly nymphs succeed very well in aquaria and if nymphs with well-developed wing-buds are taken about June or July the wonderful transformation to the imago may readily be observed. Sticks or reed stems should, of course, be placed in the aquarium to enable the nymphs to leave the water when they are ready to emerge.

Figures **282, 288** and **293** illustrate (natural size) the three types of nymph—the long and short-bodied anisopterids (dragonflies) and the slender-bodied zygopterid (damselfly) types. The individual species possessing these types of nymphs closely resemble one another and their identification is based largely on differences in the form of the mask, the shape of the two small processes on the upper surface of the base of the fore-legs where present, and in some zygopterids, the anal gills, as shown.

Long-bodied nymphs

Aeshna grandis (**282**). Whole nymph with (left) leg-base process and (right) mask (magnified). Chestnut brown or olive green, mottled. Maximum size 43 mm.

Anax imperator (**283**). Mask and leg-base process; body yellow-brown, green mottled. Size 54 mm.

Aeshna juncea (**284**). Ditto. Uniform dark brown. Size 43 mm.

Aeshna cyanea (**285**). Ditto. Sepia-brown, mottled with green. Size 48 mm.

Cordulegaster boltonii (**286**). Ditto. Sepia-brown, hairy. Size 41 mm.

Brachytron pratense (**287**). Ditto. Brown tinged with green, mottled. Size 40 mm.

Short-bodied nymphs

Libellula quadrimaculata (**288**). Whole nymph with mask and detail of movable hook on the mask. Sepia-brown above with yellowish white below. Size 25 mm.

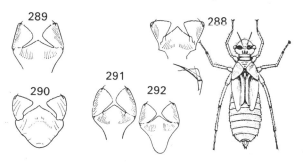

Libellula depressa (**289**). Mask. Body: sepia-brown, mottled and hairy. Size 25 mm.

Orthetrum coerulescens (**290**). Ditto. Red brown, hairy. Size 19 mm.

Sympetrum striolatum (**291**). Ditto. Pale to dark brown, spiny. Size 18 mm.

Sympetrum scoticum (**292**). Ditto. Uniform dark brown. Size 15 mm.

Slender-bodied nymphs

Agrion virgo (**293**). Whole nymph, mask and single claw (palpus) of mask. Brown or green. Size 32 mm.

Agrion splendens (**294**). Mask. Brown, grey or green. Size 32 mm.

Lestes sponsa (**295**). Ditto. Reddish brown. Size 26 mm.

Pyrrhosoma nymphula (**296**). Ditto. Dark brown. Size 20 mm.

Ischnura elegans (**297**). Ditto. Brown or green. Size 20 mm.

Enallagma cyathigerum (**298**). Mask and anal gill. Bright green. Size 20 mm.

Coenagrion puella (**299**). Ditto. Yellow-green.

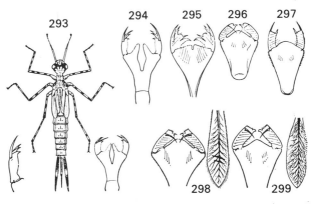

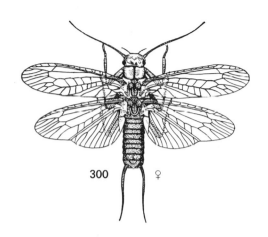

300　　　　♀

Stoneflies

The nymphs of stoneflies are found mainly under stones in fast-flowing streams or at the margins of lakes. They may be recognized by having two long tail appendages, and by their somewhat sluggish, crawling motion when disturbed, which has earned them the name 'creepers.'

The adults resemble the nymphs very closely in appearance but, of course, they have wings. They are to be found on waterside vegetation and on stones in water in summer, but they fly little. The females deposit their eggs in the water and the nymphal stage may last as long as three years in some species. In early summer hundreds of empty nymphal skins may be seen attached to stones or tree trunks along suitable stretches of water. There are 34 species of stoneflies in Britain.

Adult stonefly, *Perla bipunctata* (**300**), is a large species widespread in stony streams; length about 30 mm.

Stonefly nymphs

Isoperla grammatica (**301**), is a very common species in fast

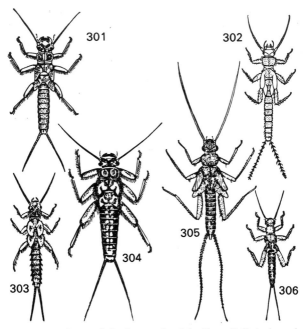

stony streams; adult the anglers' 'yellow Sally'; length about 15 mm.

Leuctra geniculata (**302**), is fairly common in slower streams; adult the anglers' 'willow fly'; length about 10 mm.

Chloroperla torrentium (**303**), is very common in stony streams; length about 8 mm.

Perla bipunctata (**304**), length up to 30 mm.

Nemurella picteti (**305**), is fairly common in slower streams and lakes; length about 8 mm.

Capnia bifrons (**306**), is fairly common under stones at the margins of lakes and in slower rivers; length about 8 mm.

Water bugs

Bugs are members of the order Hemiptera, and all the water bugs belong to the the sub-order Heteroptera, the members of which have typically the front wings modified into horny sheaths and only the hind wings membranous. Completely wingless forms occur, however, in some species of water bugs. Bugs possess a sucking beak called a rostrum with which most of them pierce their prey and suck out its juices. They retain the same general form, but not of course size, from the time they hatch from the egg until they are full grown.

Surface-film dwellers

Water cricket, *Velia caprai* (**307**), is common and widely distributed on running and still waters; occasional winged specimens occur.

Water measurer, *Hydrometra stagnorum* (**308**), is common and widely distributed, mainly on still water.

Pond skaters, *Gerris*, 8 species and *Aquarius*, 2 species (**309**) mostly widely distributed; winged and wingless forms.

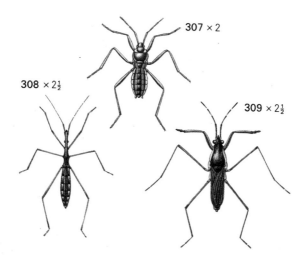

307 × 2

308 × 2½

309 × 2½

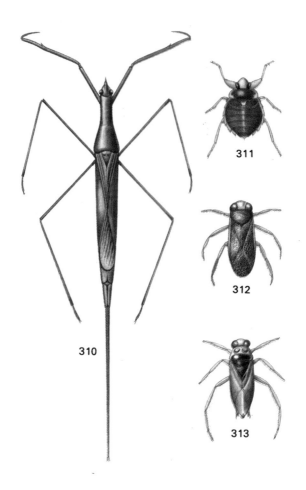

310

311

312

313

Water bugs (1½ times natural size)

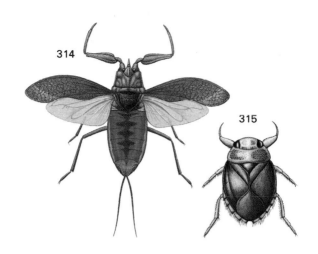

Water bugs (1½ times natural size)

Underwater dwellers

Long water scorpion, *Ranatra linearis* (**310**), is fairly common in the south, found among water plants in ponds.

Aphelocheirus montandoni (**311**), lives among the stones in rivers or lakes, often in deep water.

Lesser water boatman, *Corixa* (**312**), 4 species; swim back uppermost and body less pointed than *Notonecta;* found in ponds, lakes and rivers, feeding mostly on detritus sucked up by the rostrum.

Water scorpion, *Nepa cinerea* (**314**), is widely distributed and common in shallow water near the margins of ponds, either on the mud or among water plants; the tail spine is a breathing tube.

Water boatman, *Notonecta* (**313**), 4 species; swim generally upside down.

Ilyocoris cimicoides (**315**), is fairly common and widely distributed; occurs among water plants in still waters.

Alderflies and spongeflies

Around the margins of ponds, lakes and rivers in May and June a dullish insect, about 25 mm long, with dark brown heavily veined wings may be found, either resting on the vegetation or making short heavy flights from one perch to another. This is the alderfly, *Sialis lutaria* (**316–18**). The females lay their eggs in clusters on waterside plants and there may be up to 2,000 of the little cigar-shaped eggs in a single cluster. The minute larvae, on hatching, fall and make their way to the water, where in the mud they live for about two years, capturing and devouring with their powerful jaws any small creature they encounter. When full-grown the larvae are about 25 mm long and are usually recognized by the seven pairs of up-turned tracheal gills on the abdomen. Eventually the larvae leave the water and pupate in an oval cell in the mud nearby, emerging as winged insects in about three weeks' time.

The rarer species, *S. fuliginosa,* is darker in colour with wings almost black.

316 Alderfly

317 eggs of alderfly

318 Alderfly larva

The spongeflies (order Neuroptera, genus *Sisyra*), of which three species occur in Britain, are small insects, the larvae of which (**319**) live inside freshwater sponges (**126**) and suck their body-fluids. After a few weeks they leave the water and spin silken cocoons on surrounding vegetation. If it is early in the season, they pupate straight away and emerge as adult flies in late summer. Others, however, remain in the cocoon as larvae throughout the winter and pupate in spring, becoming adult about May. The larvae are about 5 mm long when full grown.

319

Another member of the same order, *Osmylus fulvicephalus* (**320**), is also found in or near water in the larval stage, often among mosses at the water's edge. It is about 15 mm when full-grown, dark greyish or brownish, and with a

320 Adult *Osmylus fulvicephalus*

body tapering towards the head and tail. At the tail end are a pair of finger-like appendages, which are covered with recurved hooks. The jaws are in the form of slightly curved hollow spears, with which they pierce their prey— bloodworms and other dipterous larvae—and suck their blood. The yellowish silken cocoons are found among moss in late April or early May.

China mark moths

The china mark moths are unique among British Lepidoptera in passing their immature stages under water. Five species, all belonging to the family Pyralidae, the pyralid moths, occur in Britain and although common insects they are frequently overlooked and have, as a consequence, been somewhat neglected by naturalists.

They are all fairly small moths with light-coloured wings, and their common name has been given because of the colour patterning on some of them which is supposed to resemble the potters' marks on the underside of china. They are on the wing on summer evenings, usually resting during the day near the water's edge. A gentle beating of the waterside vegetation with a stick will, however, soon dislodge them.

Still waters with floating-leaved plants such as the water-lilies, frogbit or floating pondweed growing in them are almost certain to produce the moths or their larvae. The eggs are laid on the undersides of the floating leaves and at first the young caterpillars move into the tissues of the plant, obtaining in that way both food and shelter. Later some kind of protective case is made, usually from pieces of leaf joined together with a silken secretion. The neat oval holes in water-lily leaves, made by the larvae of the brown china mark (**329**) must have puzzled many owners of garden lily-pools. If the larval cases of some of the species are opened as the caterpillars are becoming full grown, the creatures will be found to be quite dry, although living totally submerged.

During the winter when the vegetation has died down, the caterpillars are inactive and more investigations are needed on this stage of their life histories. About April, with the return of the food supply, the caterpillars become active again, and shortly afterwards they pupate, either above or below the surface depending on the species. The adult insects are on the wing from June to August.

Beautiful china mark, *Paraponyx stagnata* (**321**), is a common and widely distributed species found around the margins of lakes and rivers. It is on the wing in July and August. The larva feeds on submerged plants including bur-reed and water lilies, at first mining into their tissues, but later making a case out of two pieces of leaf joined together. It pupates in a white cocoon attached to a leaf, partially or wholly submerged.

Small china mark, *Cataclysta lemnata* (**322**), is common near ponds with duckweed on the surface. The moth is to be seen from June to August. The larval case is made from duckweed fronds and the pupal cocoon (**327**) is also covered with the fronds, and is found just below the surface. Brown china mark, *Elophila (Nymphula) nymphaeata* (**323**), is very common throughout Britain near waters where there are floating leaves. It is on the wing from June to August. The larva at first mines into the underside of a floating leaf and later makes a flat, oval case (**329**) from pieces of the leaf of floating pondweed, frogbit, water-lily, etc, attaching the case to the underside of the food plant when feeding. The pupal cocoon, covered with pieces of leaf, is attached to a stem or leaf, above or below the surface.

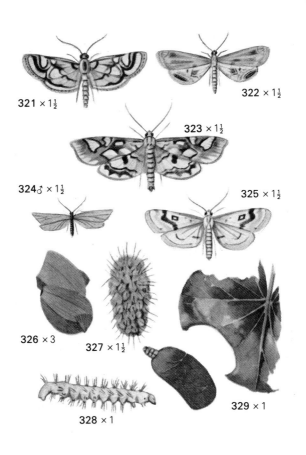

$321 \times 1\frac{1}{2}$

$322 \times 1\frac{1}{2}$

$323 \times 1\frac{1}{2}$

$324♂ \times 1\frac{1}{2}$

$325 \times 1\frac{1}{2}$

326×3

$327 \times 1\frac{1}{2}$

328×1

329×1

China mark moths and larval cases: **326** *Acentria nivea,*
329 *Elophila (Nymphula) nymphaeata;* **327** pupal case of
Cataclysta lemnata; **328** larva of *Paraponyx stratiotata*

False caddis fly, *Acentria nivea* (**324**), is a species in which the wings of the female are usually rudimentary, although a winged form occurs occasionally. The males are fairly common around still waters, including stagnant regions of rivers, appearing from July to September. The females remain underwater and pairing takes place at the surface. The larvae make loose cases (**326**) among submerged plants and pupation takes place below water level.

Ringed china mark *Paraponyx stratiotata* (**325**), is a widely distributed species which is fairly common in the south, appearing from June to August. The larva (**328**) joins leaves and stems of water plants together to make an open shelter and pupation takes place in a large oval cocoon fastened along its length to a submerged stem.

Caddis flies

Although usually overlooked, caddis flies are common insects near both still and running water habitats, flying at dusk, and remaining among the waterside vegetation during the day. By the uninitiated they might be mistaken for moths but they are not related to those insects, and on close examination it would be seen that their wings, instead of being covered with minute scales, as are those of moths and butterflies, are membranous and hairy. At rest, too, they hold their wings differently, in such a way that they form a ridge or roof over the body.

About 190 species are known in Britain, but it is probable that this number will be increased as the closer study now being given to the order begins to bear fruit. Unfortunately the larval stages of many species have yet to be described and related to the adult insects, a task in which amateur naturalists might well give valuable assistance by rearing larvae (which are easy to find and live well in captivity) to the adult stage.

Adult caddis flies—the sedge flies of the fly fisherman—have only short lives. Their mouth parts are atrophied and at the most are only capable of sipping liquids such as the nectar of flowers. The females of some species lay their eggs in the water, either descending below the surface to deposit them on stones or plants or possibly dropping them in as they fly over. On the other hand, in other species, the eggs are fastened to overhanging vegetation and the larvae, on hatching, fall into the water. The eggs are surrounded by jelly which expands in the water and serves to keep the eggs in a mass, and probably protects them from the unwelcome attentions of hungry creatures.

Caddis flies fly at dusk and during the daytime may be found by beating the branches of trees near the water. In exposed places where trees are scarce or absent, the undersides of stones near the water's edge are usually productive sites.

Phryganea varia (**330**), is found near still waters, often resting on tree trunks where it is easily overlooked on account of its similar colouring; on the wing June to August.

Grey sedge, *Odontocerum albicorne* (**331**), is widely distributed, occurring near lakes and tarns in July and August.

Sand fly, *Rhyacophila dorsalis* (**332**), is common and widely distributed near running water; June to September.

Halesus radiatus (**333**), is widely distributed near running waters; on the wing in autumn.

Large red sedge, *Phryganea striata* (**334**), is a common species near slow streams, lakes and mountain tarns; June and July.

Philopotamus montanus (**335**), is common near swift streams, appearing as early as April and abundant until autumn.

Hydropsyche instabilis (**336**), is common and widely distributed near swift-flowing waters; July and August.

Stenophylax sequax (**337**), is found near small swift streams.

Limnephilus rhombicus (**338**), is a very common species near still water in summer.

Cinnamon sedge, *Limnephilus lunatus* (**339–40**), is a

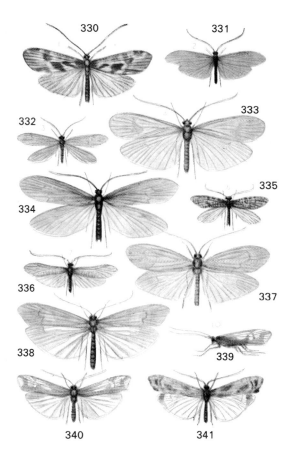

Caddis flies (natural size)

common and widely distributed species in autumn near still waters and rivers.

Glyphotaelius pellucidus (**341**), is a widely distributed species near still waters; on the wing in early summer and again in late summer.

Caddis larvae

The larvae are the well-known caddis grubs or 'worms,' familiar to all who have indulged in pond hunting, on account of the protective cases that they make from sticks, stones, leaves and other materials. Not all species make cases, however, and in running water there are a number that make at the most a silken net, usually with its open end facing up-stream, which serves the double purpose of anchoring the larva, and of trapping prey washed down by the current. This type of larva is mainly carnivorous, whereas the case-builders are generally vegetarian, although they do, on occasions, take animal food.

The cases all have as their bases an inner tube of silk spun from the head end of the caddis larva. To this the leaves or other materials are fixed, first being cut, if necessary, into the right length by the powerful jaws. New material is added from time to time at the head end, and the rear end is kept closed except for a small aperture which just allows water to flow through. Species living in still water make use mainly of plant material, which is light and buoyant, but those inhabiting fast streams either attach heavy stones to the cases or anchor the cases to large stones to avoid being swept away by the current.

The larvae have, at the tail end, two strong hooks with which they hold the inner silken tube. Along the body are tracheal gills, with which oxygen can be extracted from the water, and by rhythmic undulation the larvae keep a current of water passing through the case.

The pupal stage
After a series of moults, the larva becomes full grown and ready to pupate. If it is a free caddis (that is, without a case in the larval stage) it now constructs a shelter or

case; if it already has a case it seals up the open end with a grating which will keep out foes and yet admit a water current which it still creates by undulations of the body. The pupa is provided with a pair of strong jaws to bite its way out of this grating when it is ready to change into the winged state, and also hooks along its back to help it to get out of the case. The legs, too, are fringed with hairs and serve as very efficient oars with which to swim to the surface. Eventually either at the surface, or on land, the winged caddis fly emerges from the pupal skin and flies away.

Cases of caddis larvae

The type of case, and the materials chosen by the different species of caddis larvae, are sufficiently characteristic for identification to be carried out with a fair degree of certainty, and details of the larvae themselves are therefore excluded from this book.

The following are found mainly in still or slow-moving waters:

Triaenodes bicolor (**342**), is a common and widely distributed species in still water. The larva swims readily through the water, using its long and well-fringed legs to propel it.

Limnephilus flavicornis (**343–5**) is found in ponds, lakes

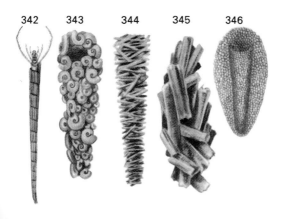

342   343   344   345   346

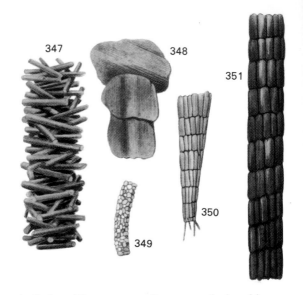

347

348

351

350

349

and ditches. Three types of cases made by this very common and widely distributed species are shown.

Molanna angustata (**346**) is made of sand grains and consists of a shield-shaped base to which the actual case is fixed. A widely distributed species, found in pools, lakes and slow streams where there is a sandy bottom.

Limnephilus rhombicus (**347**) is a large species inhabiting lakes, ponds and slow rivers. It is common and well distributed. The case consists usually of pieces of roots cut into regular lengths, but occasionally shells of water snails are added.

Glyphotaelius pellucidus (**348**) is found in ponds and the margins of lakes. The case of this common species is made of almost circular pieces of dead leaves.

Setodes argentipunctellus (**349**) is locally abundant in lakes, pools and rivers. The case is made of sand grains.

Oligotrichia ruficrus (**350**) is found in deep, weedy ponds, and the case is made of fragments of the leaves of water plants.

Phryganea grandis (**351**) is a large species found in lakes, ponds and slow rivers. It is widely distributed. The case is made of leaf fragments arranged spirally and is often very colourful. The adult is the large red sedge (**334**).

The following occur in running water, although some are also found in still water.

Anabolia nervosa (**352**) is a widely distributed and common species found both in running and still water. The tube is made of sand grains and attached to it are long pieces of stick. The adult is called the brown sedge.

Arthripsodes aterrimus (**353**) is widely distributed in both running and still water. The adult is the black silverhorns of the fly-fisherman.

Lepidostoma hirtum (**354**) is widely distributed. The case is made of leaf fragments arranged in a characteristic box-like manner.

Silo pallipes (**355**) is a common and widely distributed species, found in small fast streams. The case is made of sand grains to which are attached several larger stones.

352   353   354

355

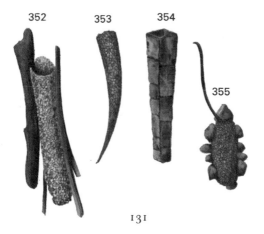

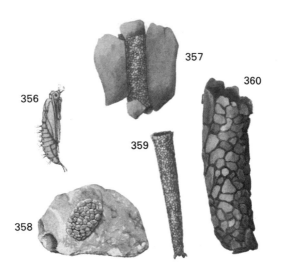

This is one of the species sometimes parasitized by an ichneumon fly, *Agriotypus armatus* (**384**), which lays its eggs inside the cases. The larvae which emerge from the eggs devour the caddis grubs and then pupate, spinning first the long filament shown in the illustration (**355**), the purpose of which is to keep the pupa within the case supplied with oxygen until it is ready to emerge as an adult.

Goera pilosa (**357**); pupa (**356**) is a very common species in rivers and the wave-washed margins of lakes. The adult is the medium sedge of the fly-fisherman. The case is another example of a tube made of sand grains to which are attached large stones (cf. *Silo pallipes*).

Agapetus fuscipes (**358**) is probably the commonest stream caddis. The little cases, made of small stones, and attached to larger stones or boulders are very numerous in streams.

Sericostoma personatum (**359**) is a common stream species, the adult of which is known as the Welshman's button.

The case is made of sand grains, very smooth and with a slight curve in it.

Potamophylax latipennis (**360**) is a common and widely distributed species, found in running water. The cases, which are made of particles of gravel, are often attached to large stones.

Two-winged flies

This huge order, Diptera, includes the house-fly, blue-bottle, gnats and midges, all insects characterized by two membranous wings, the hind pair being reduced to mere vestiges called halteres. Many kinds have aquatic larvae and pupae but none is aquatic in the adult stage. They are classified into three major groups: NEMATO-CERA—adults with long, many-jointed antennae, and larvae with well-developed heads and biting mandibles; BRACHYCERA—adults with short antennae, and larvae with incompletely developed heads which can be withdrawn into the first segment of the body; CYCLOR-RHAPHA—larva of maggot-type: larval skin remaining as protective case for pupa.

The majority of aquatic Diptera belong to the first group Nematocera and include the crane-flies; the tiny moth-flies, Psychodidae, abundant near sewage farms; the midges, gnats and mosquitoes; and the black flies, Simulidae.

Of the sub-order Brachycera the soldier-flies, Stratio-myidae, are the best-known kinds with aquatic larvae and pupae.

Cyclorrhapha is represented in fresh water only by a few species, the larvae and pupae of hover-flies and drone-flies, of which the rat-tailed maggot, *Eristalis* (**368**), is the most familiar.

Fly larvae and pupae

The terrestrial larvae of crane-flies are the familiar 'leather-jackets.' Several species, however, pass their larval stages in the mud or under stones in streams, and in the damp earth nearby. They are large fat grub-like creatures, yellowish-white in colour. Two genera, *Tipula* and *Pedicia*, are illustrated:

Tipula (**361**) has a plate bearing spiracles and surrounded by six or eight tube-like appendages on the last segment of the abdomen. The pupae have long respiratory 'horns.'

Pedicia (**362**) has no spiracular plate and there are four pairs of false legs on segments 4 to 7. Larvae of *Dicranota* have five pairs of false legs on segments 3 to 7, each ending in a circlet of hooks.

Ptychoptera (**363**), in larva form, lives buried in the mud of shallow ponds, their long extensible breathing-tube reaching to the surface of the water. In the pupa (**364**) the breathing-tube is on the head.

Soldier-fly, *Stratiomys* (**365**), in larva form, hangs suspended from the surface-film by the feathery tuft at the tail end of the body. Pupation takes place in the larval skin.

Midge, *Chironomus* (**367**), in larva form, is the well-known 'bloodworm' and is very common in ponds. There are many species, some living in the mud, some in plant tissues and others swimming freely. Pupa (**366**).

Drone-fly, *Eristalis* (**368**), in larva form is the familiar 'rat-tailed maggot' found in the black mud of the shallow parts of ponds rich in decomposing matter. The long breathing-tube is extensible and reaches to the surface of the water. Pupation takes place in the larval skin and the puparium bears two short 'horns' near the front.

Phalacrocera (**369**) is the strange larva of another genus of crane-fly, found among the sphagnum moss in bog pools.

Midge, *Dixa*, larva (**371**) and pupa (**370**) can be found in ponds among the vegetation near the surface.

Midge, *Chaoborus*, 'phantom larva' (**372**) and pupa (**373**), lives in lakes, ponds and shady pools.

Mosquito, *Culex*, larva (**374**) and pupa (**375**), is found in still waters including water-butts etc. The larvae of the related genus *Aedes* are similar; the adults are the most likely biters of man outdoors.

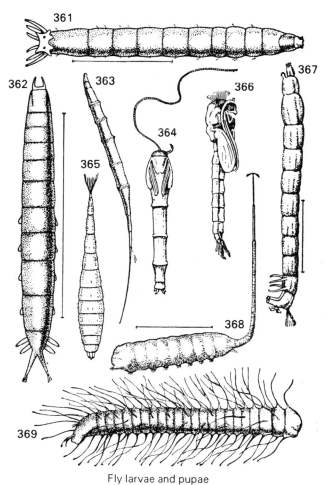

Fly larvae and pupae

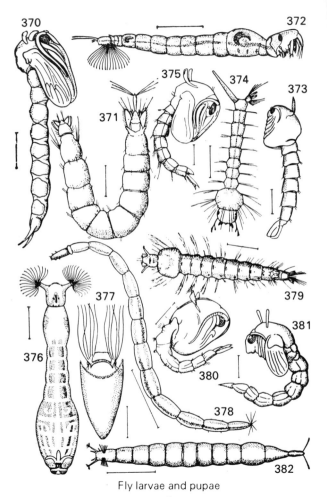

Fly larvae and pupae

Black-fly, *Simulium*, larva (**376**) and pupa (**377**), are found attached to stones and plants at the margins of streams.

Biting-midge, *Ceratopogon*, larva (**378**), is found in ponds and lakes.

Mosquito, *Anopheles*, larva (**379**) and pupa (**380**); larva is distinguished from culicine larvae by absence of a breathing-tube and by floating parallel to the water surface when at rest. It occurs mainly in southern England and fen districts.

Midge, *Tanypus*, larva (**382**) and pupa (**381**), can be found in ponds. The larva swims with vigorous serpentine movements.

Ichneumon flies and chalcid wasps

These very small insects belong to the same order as bees, wasps and ants. The female of the ichneumon fly, *Agriotypus armatus* (**384**), which is about 12 mm long, crawls into the water and lays her eggs inside the cases of caddis larvae of the genera *Goera, Silo* and *Odontocerum*. The further development of the parasites is mentioned on page 132. Three genera of chalcid wasps, commonly called fairy flies and about 1 mm long, are parasites of various aquatic insects including dragonflies, water bugs, beetles and fly larvae. The female *Caraphractus cinctus* (formerly *Polynema natans*) swims under water in search of the eggs of water beetles, using her wings as paddles. Both sexes of *Prestwichia* (**383**) live under water and swim using their legs. They parasitize the eggs of water bugs and beetles. The females of *Diapria* attack the rat-tailed larvae of the drone fly *Eristalis*.

383

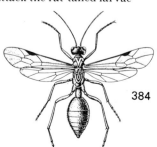

384

Water beetles

The true water beetles belong to four families of the suborder ADEPHAGA, the members of which are carnivorous in both their larval and adult stages, and one family of the POLYPHAGA, which includes both carnivorous and vegetarian beetles. Most water beetles are aquatic in both their adult and larval stages although the pupal stage is usually passed out of the water.

The characteristic feature of beetles in general is, of course, the modification of the fore pair of wings into hard and horny sheaths, or elytra, serving as protective sheaths for the membranous hind wings. The latter are not, therefore, usually visible, although perfectly functional, and it frequently comes as a surprise to the uninitiated to find that beetles can fly, particularly those that live in water. But fly they do and some species, including the great diving beetle, *Dytiscus marginalis* (**391, 393, 417**), readily leave the pond in which they are living, usually at night, and indulge in long flights in search possibly of new feeding places, during the course of which they occasionally come to grief by mistaking the roof of a greenhouse or a wet road for a stretch of water.

The eggs of water beetles are most frequently laid on the surface or in incisions made in submerged plants, but members of the family Hydrophilidae spin elaborate floating egg-cases of silk.

The larvae display great variety of form in the different species and are not easy to name, particularly as many have not yet been identified with the adult stages. The selection illustrated however, includes the types most commonly found.

When full grown, the larvae usually leave the water and make cells in the adjoining mud in which to pupate. Other species, as, for instance, the whirligig beetles, *Gyrinus* (**392**), spin silken cocoons on aerial leaves of a water plant.

Adult water beetles

Mud dweller, *Ilybius ater* (**385**), is a common species in

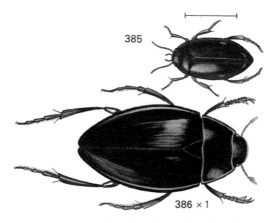

385

386 × 1

stagnant waters and it is found occasionally also in peaty water and brackish pools.

Great silver beetle, *Hydrophilus piceus* (**386, 387**), a fine insect, is found in weedy ponds and ditches, and feeds on water plants. The male is distinguishable from the female by the end joints of the tarsi (feet) of the front leg, which are flattened to form triangular plates.

387   Egg-case of the great silver beetle

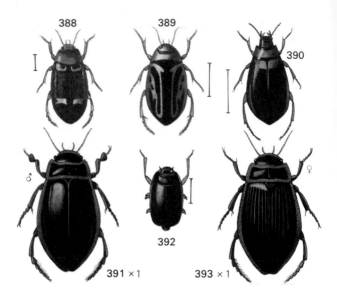

388 389 390

♂

392

391 × 1   393 × 1   ♀

Laccophilus variegatus (**388**), is a species found in drainage dykes, mainly in the south of England.

Platambus maculatus (**389**), a handsome insect, is found mainly among submerged vegetation at the margins of running water.

Screech beetle, *Hygrobia hermanni* (**390**), is a beetle which announces its presence in a collecting net by a loud squeak, a noise made by rubbing its wing covers against the end of the abdomen. A common species in muddy ponds.

Whirligig beetle, *Gyrinus natator* (**392**) may be seen swimming rapidly about in endless gyrations on the surface of still water in larger numbers, particularly in late summer.

Great diving beetle, *Dytiscus marginalis* (**391, 393**), is a common insect in ponds in all parts of Britain. It is fiercely carnivorous, often attacking prey much larger than itself,

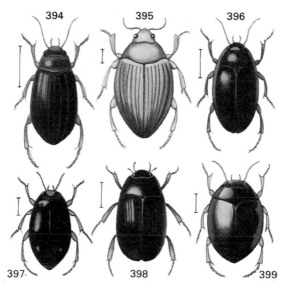

and as a consequence it is often a pest in garden pools where it will damage or destroy the fish.

Rantus pulverosus (**394**) is a species found in ponds and ditches with plenty of vegetation.

Haliplus flavicollis (**395**) is a widely distributed species found in both still and running water.

Agabus uliginosus (**396**) favours grassy pools with soft muddy bottoms.

Hydroporus erythrocephalus (**397**) is a common beetle found in boggy and marshy habitats, including salt-marshes.

Hydrobius fuscipes (**398**) is a species resembling a small Great Silver Beetle; common in still water.

Hyphydrus ovatus (**399**) is a widely distributed species, this beetle favours ponds, lakes or the stiller regions of rivers where there is a muddy bottom and plenty of vegetation.

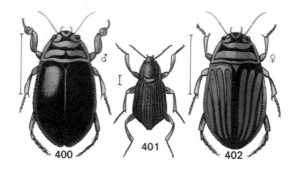

400 401 402

Acilius sulcatus (**400, 402**), a common and widely distributed species, is found in ponds, particularly those with sandy bottoms.

Elmis aenea (**401**), a small beetle, is found under stones in streams during the daytime, but it becomes more active at night and crawls on the bottom of the stream or among the submerged plants.

Beetle larvae

Acilius sulcatus (**403**) is a relative of the great diving beetle, *Dytiscus marginalis*, but the larva is distinguished by the very long first segment of the thorax.

Hygrotus parallelogrammus (**404**), brackish and fresh water.

Haliplus ruficollis (**405**) is found among filamentous algae on which plants they feed.

Hygrobia hermanni, screech beetle (**406**).

Elmis aenea (**407**) is to be found under stones in running water.

Agabus conspersus (**408**) is very common in ponds.

Hyphydrus ovatus (**409**), whose pronounced 'snout' is a distinguishing feature of this larva, is common in ponds.

Helodes minuta (**410**) is found under stones in running water. The rarer *H. marginata* is similar but about 1 cm.

Ilybius fenestratus (**411**).

Dytiscus marginalis, great diving beetle (**412**), is a fiercely carnivorous larva, readily identified when full grown by its large size.

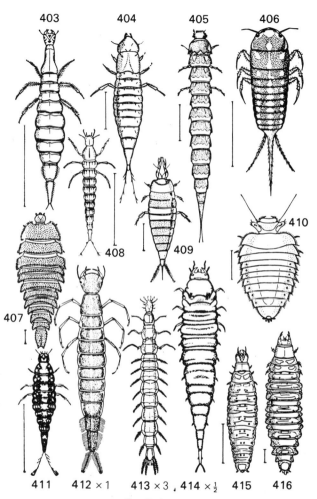

Beetle larvae

143

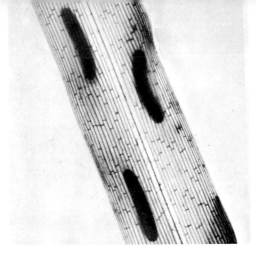

417 Eggs of diving beetle in the stem of a water plant

Gyrinus sp., whirligig beetle (**413**), has a pair of hair-like tracheal gills on each segment of the abdomen except the last, which has two pairs. 10 species occur in Britain, the commonest probably being *G. natator.*

Hydrophilus piceus, great silver beetle (**414**) the largest water beetle larva, is found in weedy ditches and ponds and feeds on water-snails.

Hydrobius fuscipes (**415**), which is common in still water, has four teeth on each mandible.

Laccobius minutus (**416**) is an acid-water species.

ARACHNIDS

Most arachnids are land dwellers, but the two best known groups, spiders and mites, have representatives in fresh water.

Water spider

This is the only truly aquatic member of the order Araneae, although a number of other spiders frequent the

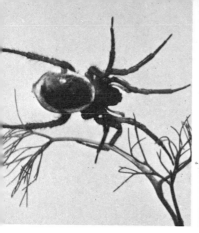

418 Male water spider
Argyroneta aquatica

419 Airbell

waterside (**418**). It is found in weedy ponds and ditches
and spins a bell-shaped web (**419**) among water plants
which holds a large air-bubble and it is in this that the
spider spends most of its time and where, in an upper
compartment, the female lays her 50–100 eggs. The
female spider is about 10 mm long and the male slightly
larger. Small animals are caught and taken back to the
bell to eat.

Water mites

Water mites are common in most freshwater habitats.
Some species swim actively in the water whereas others
are sluggish and crawl about on the mud. Although they
are small creatures, most of them are brightly coloured
and thus easily seen.

The females of some species lay their eggs in jelly-like
masses on submerged plants or stones, but others insert
them into punctures made in water plant stems. The
larvae are parasitic on other water creatures and may

sometimes be found in considerable numbers attached to aquatic insects. When fully developed the larvae drop off their hosts and become free-living mites.

Water mites are carnivorous and suck out the body fluids of their prey through their pointed beaks. About 320 species are found in Britain. A few common species are illustrated here.

Family Limnocaridae

Hydrodroma despiciens, female (**420**), is a very common species in ponds; length 2 mm.

Limnochares aquatica, female (**421**), is a creeping species, found in the mud of ponds, lakes and canals; length 4 mm.

Diplohydrachna globosa, female (**422**); various species of this genus are common and their larvae are the ones most frequently found attached to water bugs or beetles; length 2–3 mm.

Great diving beetle, *Dytiscus marginalis* (**423**), with many larvae of *D. globosa* attached.

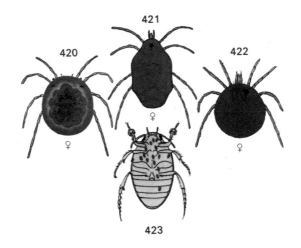

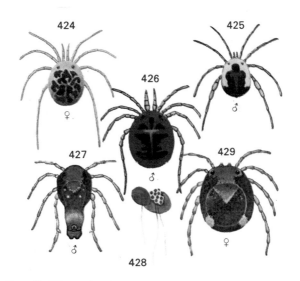

Family Hygrobatidae

Hygrobates longipalpis, female (**424**); length 2 5 mm.
Neumania spinipes, male (**425**); length 1 mm.
Limnesia fulgida, male (**426**); length 1·8 mm.
Megaluracarus buccinator, male (**427**); length 1·2 mm;
female (**429**); length 1·2 mm.

Eggs of *Hygrobates longipalpis* on duckweed (**428**).

WATER BEARS

These very small animals, less than a millimetre long,
were formerly considered to be related to the arachnids,
but are now considered to be direct descendants of the
ancestors of the arthropods and occupy a phylum all to
themselves. They resemble minute bears with eight
stumpy legs bearing hooks at their ends (**430**). They suck
the cell contents of plants through piercing mouth-parts,
and are found in the damp vegetation at the edge of fresh

430 Water
bear

waters, among mosses or liverworts and also in the detritus
of ponds and lakes. If their surroundings dry up, they can
exist in a state of suspended animation for long periods.
74 species have been recorded in the British Isles.

VERTEBRATES

Although the invertebrates, or animals without backbone,
form the bulk of the creatures encountered in observing
and studying pond life, no review of the subject would be
complete without a brief mention of the vertebrates
occurring in freshwater which include the lampreys, the
fish and the amphibians.

LAMPREYS

Two species occur in Britain: the river lamprey, *Lampetra
fluviatilis,* and the brook lamprey, *Lampetra planeri.* The
former may reach a length of 50 cm whereas the brook
lamprey rarely exceeds a size of 25 cm. At first glance
they may be mistaken for eels but their lack of jaws, their
sucker mouth and the gill-clefts along the body behind
the head distinguish them. They both feed on smaller
creatures such as crustaceans, insect larvae and occasionally on fish, to which they attach themselves by means of
their sucker mouth.

FISH

Space precludes descriptions of all the species of freshwater
fish and the reader is referred for detailed information to
another volume in this series dealing exclusively with

fish. Representatives of many families occur in ponds, lakes and streams, and freshwater fish do not form a separate group. The most handsome and best known are members of the *Salmonidae*—the salmon, trout, char and grayling, inhabitants mainly of running water or lakes. The majority of the so-called 'coarse fish' belong to the *Cyprinidae*—the carp family—and include the gudgeon, tench (**434**), minnow, chub, dace, roach (**431**), bream and the carp (**435**) itself—the last probably not a native fish but a species introduced long ago for food purposes.

One of our handsomest fishes is the perch (**433**), which with the smaller pope or ruffe, represent the family *Percidae*. In larger ponds, lakes and slow rivers the ferocious pike takes its toll not only of fish but also of frogs, water-voles, and even water-birds.

The common eel, a frequent inhabitant of streams and ponds, deserves mention on account of its interesting life-history. All adult eels in Europe, when ready to breed, make their way to the sea and cross the Atlantic Ocean, where in deep water there they spawn and then die. The flat, transparent larvae undertake the immense journey back to the place from which their parents came, taking up to three years to reach their destinations.

In rapid streams may be found a little fish beautifully adapted for life in running water, the bullhead or miller's-thumb. Its flattened body enables it to remain hidden between, or even under stones, waiting for the smaller fish or other prey which are instantly snapped up when they come within range. In such habitats, too, lives the unrelated stone loach, easily recognized by the fringe of barbels around the mouth.

Finally must be mentioned the beautiful little fish, the capture of which must start the career of many a naturalist—the three-spined stickleback, *Gasterosteus aculeatus* (**432**), whose interesting nest-building activities have endeared it to generations of nature lovers. Although mainly found in ponds and streams throughout the country, this ubiquitous little fish sometimes occurs in the brackish water of river estuaries. It feeds mainly on small

431

432

433

434

435

Freshwater fish

animal food. In spring the male builds a nest of plant fragments glued together with a secretion and in it several females lay their eggs. Size 4 to 6 cm.

Roach, *Rutilis rutilis* (**431**), is common and widespread but scarcer in Scotland and the west. Frequents ponds, slow rivers and canals where there are plenty of waterplants. Food: plants, crustaceans, insects and molluscs. Size 15 to 30 cm.

Perch, *Perca fluviatilis* (**433**), is well distributed in Britain, mainly in rivers and lakes, favouring water of medium depth. Food: mainly insects and crustaceans, although they occasionally take small fish. Size 15 to 30 cm.

Tench, *Tinca tinca* (**434**), is widespread throughout the country, inhabiting mainly slow rivers, canals and weedy lakes. They are bottom feeders and in winter often lie buried in the mud. Food: worms, molluscs and decaying plant and animal remains. Size 20 to 30 cm.

Carp, *Cyprinus carpio* (**435**), is widespread in lakes and larger ponds. Feeds mainly on the bottom on water plants, worms, crustaceans. Size 25 to 50 cm.

AMPHIBIANS

It is usually only in their breeding season in spring or early summer that the amphibians—frogs, toads, and newts—are to be found actually in the water. During the rest of the period when they are active they live in damp places on land. Their larvae, or tadpoles, are of course important members of the fauna of still waters, providing much food for the larger carnivorous creatures.

Our amphibians belong to two orders:

CAUDATA—the tailed amphibians—newts.

SALIENTA—the tailless amphibians—frogs and toads.

Newts

Britain possesses three species of newt—the common or

smooth newt (**437–8**); the palmate newt (**439–40**); and the great crested newt (**442–3**). During the greater part of the year they live on land, hiding under stones during the day and hunting for prey at night in summer and autumn, hibernating in winter. In spring, they repair to ponds, where after a short courtship, the male deposits a transparent capsule of sperms in the water which the female grasps with her vent and releases the sperms into her body to fertilize the eggs before laying them. The eggs are attached singly to water plants, enveloped in a gelatinous envelope and frequently the leaf on which an egg is laid will be bent over to shield it.

The tadpoles have three pairs of external feathery gills which are retained until the end of the larval period. The front pair of legs appear first and the hind legs follow. By the middle of August some larvae have completed their metamorphosis although many over-winter.

Adult newts feed on insects, worms and slugs.

Common or smooth newt, *Triturus vulgaris* (**436–8**), is common and widely distributed in England and eastern Scotland, local elsewhere. It also occurs in Ireland—the only newt to do so. This is the least aquatic of our three species and leaves the water soon after the breeding season is over, hiding under stones, logs and other cover during the day and seeking their prey at night. Size 10 cm.

Palmate newt, *Triturus helveticus* (**439–41**), is widely

436 Tadpole of smooth newt

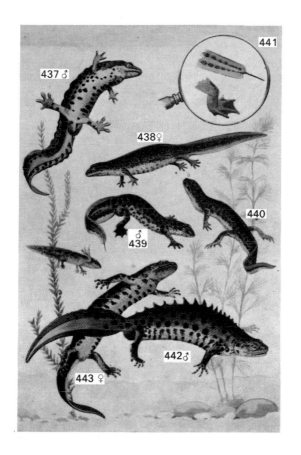

Newts

distributed in England, Scotland and Wales and commoner than is generally supposed. The male can be distinguished from the male of the preceding species by the webbed hind feet and the filament at the end of the truncated tail (**441**); both of which features are more pronounced in the breeding season. The females are difficult to distinguish from each other but *usually* the female smooth newt has a spotted throat and that of the palmate newt is without spots. Size 7·5 cm.

Great crested or warty newt, *Triturus cristatus* (**442–3**), occurs locally throughout England (except Cornwall), Scotland and Wales, preferring rather large ponds. It remains in the water longer than the other two species, sometimes all the year round. Size about 13–15 cm.

Frogs

Although the common frog (**444–5**) is the only native species, two others have been introduced to this country—the edible frog (**446–7**) and the marsh frog (**448–9**). Although the former has not increased its range much since it was introduced in parts of southern England, the marsh frog has spread somewhat from its place of introduction in the Romney Marsh area of Kent and Sussex.

Common frog, *Rana temporaria* (**444**) (tadpole **445**), is found abundantly all over Britain including Ireland, into which country it was introduced in the seventeenth century. This species is known as the grass or brown frog

444   445

447

446

448

449

on the continent. The colouring varies greatly in individuals and even albinos are known. Frogs breed as soon as they emerge from hibernation and then leave the water, living in damp places on land. The food—insects, worms, slugs, etc—is taken mainly at night. The tadpoles take about 12 weeks to complete their metamorphosis. Size about 7·5 cm.

Edible frog, *Rana esculenta* (**447**) (tadpole **446**), has been introduced to this country on a number of occasions and has persisted in a few areas of the south of England. It is more attached to water than our native frog and always lives within easy reach of it, although it also enjoys basking in the sun. Size about 7 cm male, 7·5 cm female.

Marsh frog, *Rana ridibunda* (**448**) (tadpole **449**), formerly a native of eastern Europe, was introduced into Kent in 1935 and has now spread over a wide area of Romney Marsh and adjoining districts. It keeps near to water and readily plunges on the approach of danger. Its diet may include small mammals and nestling birds. Size about 9 cm male, up to 15 cm female.

Toads

Toads can readily be distinguished from frogs by their shorter legs, which enable them to progress by crawling rather than by hopping, and by their warty skins. The common toad, too, is frequently found far from water in summer and autumn. Egg-laying takes place rather later than that of the common frog, and the eggs are in long ropes (**450**).

450
Spawn of
common
toad

The rarer natterjack toad (**451–2**) congregates in some numbers in habitats suitable for it, which are usually in sandy areas where there are pools in which to breed. The characteristic yellow stripe down the middle of the back immediately identifies this species.

Natterjack toad, *Bufo calamita* (**452**) (tadpoles **451**), is a dwindling species because of human pressures on its habitats. It prefers sandy places where it can make burrows in which to hide during the daytime. The tadpoles complete their metamorphosis rapidly in about 6 to 8 weeks. Size 6 cm.

Common toad, *Bufo bufo* (**453**) (tadpole **454**), is widely distributed and common over England, Scotland and Wales. Frequently found well away from water and often stays in one locality for a long time. The eggs are laid in strings, often 3 or 4 m long, entwined around water plants. The tadpole stage lasts 8 to 12 weeks. Size about 6 cm male, 10 cm female.

451
452
453
454

4. STUDYING POND LIFE

In recent years the disappearance of ponds, through urban and industrial development and intensive agriculture, has threatened the existence of many freshwater plants and animals and it is now important to conserve those that are left. Indiscriminate collecting must be avoided and if possible all larger specimens examined at the waterside, preferably in a large white dish, and returned as soon as possible to the pond once field notes have been made.

If some specimens are essential for further study, no more should be taken than are strictly necessary and they should be kept in cool, shady conditions in suitable containers and returned to their original habitat as soon as they have been studied.

When stones or logs are turned over in the water, to search for specimens, they must be turned back again to their original positions, otherwise the animals which live underneath may die. Water plants which have been taken out to be examined for specimens must be returned to the water and not left on the bank to rot.

Avoid trampling the ground along pond and stream margins and leave the area as you found it. Permission must always be obtained from landowners or occupiers to study on private land.

The equipment for the study of freshwater plants and animals need be neither elaborate nor expensive, and much of it can be made at home or improvised from odds and ends. The first essential is a net, and for catching larger creatures such as beetles and bugs, one made of fairly coarse material will suffice, or a metal kitchen sieve (**455**) can be used. For the collection of microscopical life, and especially the free-floating algae, a plankton-net is used. This has a bag made of fine-meshed fabric—usually

455 Household sieve used as a net

456 Collecting equipment: A weed drag; B small plankton net; C shell scoop; D weed-cutting knife (B,C and D screw on to a collecting stick); E hand-lens; F pondside trough for examining catch; G pipette; H spoon; I forceps; J camelhair paint brush (G – J are for sorting out the catch); K large enamel or porcelain dish for examining the catch.

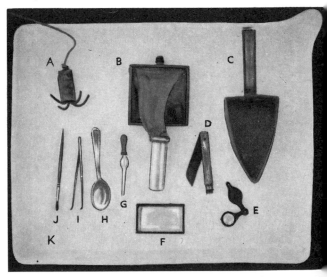

nylon today—fastened at its lower end around the rim of a small glass or plastic tube. After sweeping the net through the water a few times it is withdrawn and the organisms drain into the tube and can be given a preliminary examination with a hand-lens before emptying the sample into a tube for further study.

Although a stick is usually attached to the net, it is often necessary to obtain samples beyond the reach of even extending sticks and the net is then fastened by three short cords to a long line to enable it to be thrown as far as possible from the bank.

Dealers in natural history supplies can provide the basic equipment but some of the items illustrated (**456**) can probably be found at home or in school.

A simple draghook, for hauling water plants to the bank is a useful piece of equipment. One can be made simply by taking several pieces of strong galvanized wire about 25 cm long, bending one end of each into the form of a hook, and slipping the other ends into a short length of lead piping. If these are now bent over and the piping hammered flat, the wires will be secured. A length of strong cord, such as picture cord, attached to the drag will enable it to be tossed into the middle of a pond and then slowly hauled in, when the plants can be examined over a white enamel dish or plate or even a piece of light-coloured mackintosh.

Finally a few glass tubes and small tins (such as pastille tins); honey or fruit-preserving jars for the larger creatures; a small paint-brush and a simple fountain-pen filler type of pipette for transferring the catch, will complete the essential collecting equipment.

WORKING TO A PURPOSE

Much more point is given to pond-hunting expeditions if a systematic approach to the subject is adopted rather than the usual haphazard 'lucky dip.' An attempt might be made, for example, to find out something about the ecology of a pond (see page 161) and to find out the

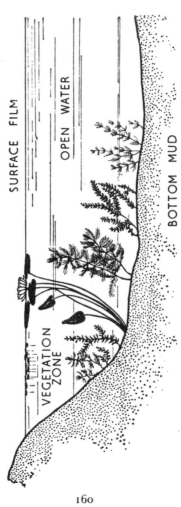

SURFACE FILM

OPEN WATER

VEGETATION ZONE

BOTTOM MUD

457 Pond zones

answers to the questions, '*What* lives *where* and *when* and *how* and *why?*' A start might be made by drawing a rough sketch map of the pond and indicating on it the extent of the plant zones, or better still by making a profile of the pond (**2**).

Then by systematic collecting in the various regions of the pond (**457**) a representative example of the animal life would be obtained. Back at home or in the classroom, a 'demonstration bench' can be set out bearing written labels of the main animal groups based on the details given on pages 51–53. On sorting out the catch each species is transferred to a separate dish or saucer and set out in its appropriate place on the demonstration bench; thus not only is a clear insight gained into classification, but an indication is given of the groups represented in the pond and those that are missing.

Having noted where the animals were found, it is then advantageous to mark their locations on the sketch map or profile. Thus dragonfly nymphs, beetle larvae, etc, would be indicated as appearing among submerged vegetation; 'bloodworms' and some annelid worms in the mud; and pond skaters and whirligig beetles on the surface film.

Carried out in this way, pond hunting begins to have some meaning; fresh problems present themselves for investigation and eventually work of real scientific value may result.

FRESHWATER ECOLOGY

In the opening pages of this book the importance to the organisms living in freshwater of such physical and chemical factors as temperature, light, dissolved gases and salts, and water movements were described. The impact of these factors varies not only between one stretch of water and another, but often between different areas, or zones, of the same pond or stream. In studying a particular body of water, and its characteristic communities of animals and plants, it is convenient to consider it as consisting of a series of zones.

Still waters

In an average pond four main zones of life may be recognized (**457**):

1 The surface-film.
2 The region of submerged and floating vegetation.
3 The open water.
4 The bottom mud.

Each of these zones has peculiar advantages and disadvantages, and consequently its own characteristic communities capable of living under the conditions.

The surface-film (**457**)   This frontier between air and water provides a habitat with adequate oxygen, abundant food in the form of small creatures that have fallen accidentally there, and comparative freedom from predators. The zone has been colonized by a number of insects that are beautifully adapted to live there—light, slender water bugs, such as the pond skater and water measurer—whose slight weight spread over a wide area by means of long legs, the tips of which sometimes bear water-repellent hairs, enables them to be supported on the surface-film. Actively swimming there are the whirligig beetles, while below, hanging from the underside of the film are the larvae and pupae of two-winged flies, such as gnats.

The zone of vegetation   From the pond margins to a distance that varies in every stretch of water is a zone of vegetation—a region of abundant food and also plentiful oxygen, derived from the photosynthesis of the plants, but with a good deal of competition among the inhabitants. Here live the greatest variety of species—beetles, both larval and adult water bugs, dragonfly and mayfly nymphs, snails, mites, leeches and flatworms.

The open water   Free-swimming or free-floating organisms form the main population of the area of open water towards the middle of the pond. These include the largest members of the fauna—the fish, and the smallest—the planktonic animals which form a large part of their food, including water fleas and rotifers.

The bottom mud This apparently unpromising zone supports nevertheless a surprisingly large number of individuals, if of few species. Food may be plentiful in the form of decaying plant and animal remains, but oxygen may be scarce. Creatures that can thrive in these conditions include the 'bloodworm' larvae of midges and annelid worms such as *Tubifex,* all possessing the red blood pigment haemoglobin which, on account of its great affinity for oxygen enables them to make the most of what little of this gas is present. Here, too, may be found bivalve molluscs, such as the orb-shell and pea-shell cockles.

Running water The zonation of a river is along its length and the various reaches will have their character-istic communities. First come the *head-streams,* the source of the river, often little more than shallow trickles with partly submerged moss or stones. These streams support a surprisingly large population of small animals among the moss-tufts or under stones—caddis larvae, flatworms, rotifers and protozoa.

The head-streams give way to a wider water-course with a stony or gravelly bed and a strong current carrying all before it. This zone is termed the *trout-beck.* Little plant-life can exist in the torrent, and such small animals as are present are flattened forms adapted for clinging to the underside of stones—the nymphs of mayflies such as *Ecdyonurus* and the stoneflies, a few caddis larvae and leeches. Trout occur in the deeper water and the miller's thumb shelters among stones.

Further on its course the river may enter a zone termed the *minnow reach* where although the current is still fast, some silting occurs in sheltered spots and a few plants, such as the water crowfoot, are able to gain a foothold, while water moss, *Fontinalis* (**95**), may also grow abun-dantly on the stones. The plants provide niches for a

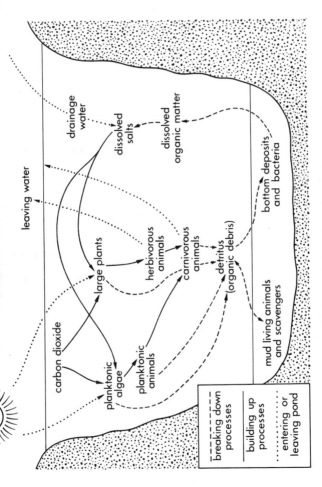

458 Inter-relation of pond organisms

drainage water

dissolved salts

dissolved organic matter

leaving water

carbon dioxide

large plants

herbivorous animals

carnivorous animals

detritus (organic debris)

bottom deposits and bacteria

planktonic algae

planktonic animals

mud living animals and scavengers

breaking down processes

building up processes

entering or leaving pond

164

variety of small creatures and caddis larvae, snails, planarian flatworms and freshwater shrimps may be among the richer animal life.

In the *lowland reach,* where the current is slow and the course meandering, much silting may take place and conditions here may be similar to those in ponds with much the same communities of animals and plants. Finally, as the river reaches the sea, estuarine conditions appear and tidal action limits the organisms to those that can tolerate a high degree of salinity. These may include some molluscs such as Jenkins' spire shell, the zebra mussel and some water shrimps.

FOOD WEBS

In fresh water, the interdependence of the living organisms (**458**) can be seen more clearly perhaps than in any other natural environment. The first links in the food-chain are, of course, the inorganic substances dissolved in the water, such as the salts of various metals (calcium, potassium, iron, etc), and the gas carbon dioxide. The green plants, both microscopic and large, can utilize these basic materials directly to build up living matter which becomes available as food for the herbivorous animals, which in turn provide nourishment for the carnivores. Every organism that is not eaten, in time dies and disintegrates, firstly into detritus, and then by bacterial activity is broken down into simpler inorganic substances once more. Thus there is a constant circulation of food material in a typical pond or lake, although the position may be complicated in a large, deep lake by the 'locking-up' of reserve materials at the bottom in summer, due to the establishment of a 'thermocline' or temperature barrier, which prevents the free inter-change of nutrient materials between the bottom and top zones of the lake.

KEYS FOR IDENTIFICATION OF SELECTED GROUPS

To use the keys, start with the first pair of alternatives and after selecting the description which applies to the specimen being examined, proceed to the next pair of alternatives indicated by number, and then repeat the process there. Eventually this should lead to the name of the animal or to its group. (It has not been possible, however, to compile such simplified artificial keys to include all the animals in particular groups.)

Flatworms

1 One pair of eye spots	2
More than one pair	5

2 Head end pointed but with no horns	3
Head end nearly square and may have horns	4
3 Head triangular; base of triangle widest part of body	*Dugesia tigrina*
Head pointed; streaks behind eyes; rounded posterior end	*Dugesia lugubris*
4 Eyes widely spaced; no horns; irregular border to head end	*Bdellocephala punctata*
Eyes close together; well-marked horns	*Crenobia alpina*

5 Large number eye spots; no horns	*Polycelis nigra*
Large number eye spots; well-marked horns	*Polycelis felina*

Segmented Worms

1 Two bristles in each bundle	2

	More than two bristles in each bundle	4
2	Bristles not cleft; clitellum present; square tail	*Eiseniella*
	Bristles in ventral bundles cleft	3
3	Distinct long narrow proboscis; dorsal bristles long	*Stylaria*
	Broad anterior end; no bristles on segments 3, 4 and 5	*Chaetogaster*
	Body greenish at anterior end; dark red blood	*Lumbriculus*
4	Ventral bristles hooked; tube dwelling with tail out	*Tubifex*
	Bristles all simple; clitellum obvious; whitish	*Lumbricillus*

Leeches

1	One pair eye spots close together	*Helobdella stagnalis*
	More than one pair eye spots	2
2	Three pairs eye spots	3
	Four or five pairs eye spots	4
3	Six rows of cream spots on body; curls up when disturbed	*Glossiphonia complanata*
	Brownish or blackish spots; carries eggs	*Glossiphonia heteroclita*
4	Four pairs eye spots	5
	Five pairs eye spots; large	*Haemopis sanguisuga*
5	Large; six rows yellowish spots; carries eggs	*Theromyzon tessulatum*
	Narrow body; blackish markings	6
6	Third pair eye spots in line	*Erpobdella testacea*
	Third pair eye spots staggered	*Erpobdella octoculata*

Molluscs

1	Univalve	2

| | Bivalve | 18 |

2 With an operculum   3
   No operculum   6

3 Shell very little higher than broad   *Valvata*
   Shell distinctly higher than broad   4

4 Operculum rather limy; concentric markings   *Bithynia*
   Operculum horny; spiral markings; retractable within aperture   5

5 Operculum with brownish tinge; 5½ whorls   *Potamopyrgus (Hydrobia) jenkinsi*

6 Shell limpet-like; apex almost median—6 mm   *Ancylus lacustris*
   Shell helically wound or coiled   7

7 Shell not coiled in one plane; spire projecting   8
   Coiled nearly in one plane   14

8 Shell sinistral and shiny   *Physa fontinalis*
   Shell dextral; broad tentacles   9

9 Tall spire   10
   Short spire   13

10 Large; last whorl very large; acute spire   *Lymnaea stagnalis*
     Medium or small; last whorl not very large; spire less acute   11

11 Small aperture about one-third shell; uneven taper   *Lymnaea glabra*
   Aperture one-half shell; even taper   12

12 Umbilicus closed by laid back lips   *Lymnaea palustris*
     Umbilicus open; flattened on top   *Lymnaea truncatula*

13 Last whorl expanded; margin reflexed outwards   *Lymnaea auricularia*

Not so expanded; no reflexion; aperture meets at less than 90° *Lymnaea pereger*

14 Very large; up to 25 mm *Planorbarius corneus*

Much smaller; 3 mm–10 mm 15
    15 Whorls strongly ridged, transversely *Planorbis crista*

        No ridges 16
    16 Whorls taller than broad; tight coil; overlapping below *Planorbis contortus*

Whorls not taller than broad; not tightly coiled 17

17 Six whorls; round or slightly angled *Planorbis spirorbis*
    Less than six whorls; spiral markings aperture rather large *Planorbis albus*

18 Large 19
    Small 20

    19 Depression in front of umbone *Unio*
        No depression *Anodonta*

    20 Umbone central; shell equilateral *Sphaerium*
        Umbone subterminal; shell inequilateral *Pisidium*

Mayfly larvae

1 Burrowing form 2
  Crawling or swimming forms 3
2 Long mandibles; two branched fringed gills; curved back *Ephemera*
3 Flattened body (usually in streams) 4
  More or less cylindrical body 5
4 Very broad and flat with flat limbs; gills not fringed *Ecdyonurus*
  Fairly broad and flat; feathery gills *Heptagenia*
  Fairly broad and flat; first pair gills large and touching ventrally *Rhithrogena*

169

	Not so broad; all gills forked and then branched	*Habrophlebia*
5	Swimming forms	6
	Crawling forms	8
6	Six pairs gills double; seventh pair single	*Clöeon*
	Seven pairs double gills	*Leptophlebia*
	Seven pairs single gills	7

	7 Middle tail shorter; labial palp rounded	*Baetis*
	Gills lanceolate; labial palp truncate	*Centroptilum*
8	Second pair of six gills large and cover the rest	*Caenis*
	Five pairs of gills	*Ephemerella*

Stonefly larvae

	1 First and second tarsals together very short and less than half third segment	2
	First and second tarsals together more than half third segment	3
2	Gill tufts on abdomen obvious; body large and robust	*Perla*
	No gill tufts; body slender	*Isoperla*
3	Second tarsal as long as first	*Taeniopteryx*
	Second tarsal shorter than first	4
4	Hind wing cases in nymph more widely divergent than the fore	*Nemoura*
	Hind wing cases in nymph parallel with fore wing cases	5
5	Pale and slender; middle abdominal segments longer than wide	*Leuctra*
	Dark-coloured; middle abdominal segments wider than long; short antennae	*Capnia*

Water bugs

1. Conspicuous antennae; mostly surface livers 4
   Very small antennae often hidden underneath; truly aquatic 2
2. Long tail tube 3
   No tail tube 6
3. Flat broad body; flattened front legs .... *Nepa*
   Long slender body and legs .... *Ranatra*

4. Hind femur extends beyond end of abdomen .... *Gerris*
   Hind femur does not extend beyond end of abdomen 5
5. Very elongated head; slender body .... *Hydrometra*
   Stouter body, conspicuous orange stripes .... *Velia*
6. Swims ventral side uppermost .... *Notonecta*
   Swims dorsal side uppermost 7
7. Head with sharp pointed beak; oval body .... *Ilyocoris*
   No sharply pointed beak .... *Corixa*

Caddis larvae

1. Larva with transportable case 2
   Free-living, net-spinning, or tunnel dwellers 8
2. Case of spirally arranged vegetable matter 3
   Case not as above 4
3. Case small, slender, carried by swimming larva .... *Triaenodes*
   Case large and not carried by swimming larva .... *Phryganea*
4. Case very small; seed or flask shaped 5
   Case medium to large 6
5. Case leathery in appearance; silk only .... *Agraylea*
   Case includes sand grains as well; light colour (3–4 mm) .... *Hydroptila*
   Case shaped like a conical flask (5 mm) .... *Oxyethira*

6	Case made of sand grains only	7
	Case made of sand grains with much larger stones cemented on sides	*Sericostoma*
	Case may include sand grains and other materials	Limnephilids
	Case of stones; flat on one side and strongly curved on other	*Agapetus*
7	Case conical and fairly strongly curved	*Arthripsodes*
	Case straight cylinder	*Potamophylax*
8	Larva inhabiting fixed tunnel on stone	9
	Larva not inhabiting fixed tunnel	10
9	Small reddish-green slender body; anal gills only; long tortuous tunnel	*Tinodes*
	Medium to large; very small head; gills in bunches on abdomen; only in tunnel in pre-pupation period	*Rhyacophila*
10	Net-spinning larva	11
	Free larvae which do not spin nets	12
11	Larva 15–18 mm; much-branched gills on underside of abdomen	*Hydropsyche*
	Larva medium size (12 mm) reddish head; uniformly broad body	*Polycentropus* or *Cyrnus*
12	Larva medium to large; very small head; gills in bunches on abdomen	*Rhyacophila*

Fly and midge larvae

1	Spiracular plate and gills on last segment	2
	No spiracular plate	4
2	Body with numerous long spines	*Phalacrocera*
	No spines	3
3	Six or eight lobes round rectangular spiracular disk	*Tipula*
	Five or less lobes; five pairs false legs	*Dicranota*
4	Seven pairs false legs; retractile tail	*Eristalis*
	Two pairs false legs	9
	None or one pair false legs	5
5	Antennae simple; retractable tail	*Ptychoptera*
	Antennae simple; mouth brush and	

posterior sucker   *Simulium*
Antennae hairy   6
6 Transparent body; four air sacs   *Chaoborus*
    No air sacs   7

    7 Worm-like;   posterior
      crown of stiff bristles   *Forcipomyia*
      Broad thoracic segments;
      breathing siphon   8

8 Hangs head down at rest   *Culex*
    Hangs parallel to water surface   *Anopheles*
9 Body held double; mouth brushes;
    false legs on abdominal segments 1
    & 2   *Dixa*

    One pair false legs on thorax and one
    on last abdominal segment   10

    10 Anterior false legs fused   11
      Anterior   false   legs   12
      distinct

11 Long slender antennae; banded
    body; small and slender   *Corynoneura*
    Short retractable antennae; body
    broader at front end   *Tanypus*
12 Four tubular and four anal gills;   *Chironomus*
    often red

Beetles

    1 Thread antennae   2
      Clubbed antennae   6
2 Large, olive brown with light brown
    edge to wings   *Dytiscus*
    Less than 25 mm long   3
3 Narrow body, black elytra with yellow
    margin streak   *Ilybius*
    Globular body, reddish   *Hyphydrus*
    Neither of above   4
4 About 12 mm long; black markings   *Acilius*
    on thorax
    Less than 12 mm   5

173

5	Elytra shiny dark red or black	*Agabus*
	Thorax yellow or yellowish black	*Laccophilus*
	Elytra brown and yellow	*Deronectes*
6	Circles on surface of water	*Gyrinus*
	Under water swimmers	7
7	Very large; silvery appearance underneath when submerged	*Hydrophilus*
	About 12 mm or less; metallic blue or green	*Hydrobius*
	Very small; poor swimmers	*Hydrophilids*

Beetle larvae

1	Two tarsal claws	2
	One tarsal claw	8
2	Two tail processes	3
	Three tail processes	9
	No definite tail process	7
3	Tail processes longer than abdomen is wide	4
	Tail processes shorter than abdomen is wide	6
4	Tail processes plumose	*Laccophilus*
	Tail processes not plumose	5
5	Head had a pronounced snout; small	*Hyphydrus*
	Head prolonged into a short beak; small	*Hydroporus or Deronectes*
6	Very long first thoracic segment; very short 'tails' processes	*Acilius*
	No 'neck'; hairy tail process; very large mandibles; larvae up to 50 mm long	*Dytiscus*
7	Four hooks at end of abdomen; abdominal gills	*Gyrinus*
	Very dark body; five white retractile gills at end of abdomen	*Helodes*
8	One obvious tail process	*Haliplus*
	No tail process	*Hydrophilus*
9	Large head; three hairy tail processes	*Hygrobia*

BOOKS FOR FURTHER READING

General Works

J. Clegg, *Freshwater Life* (Wayside and Woodland series), Frederick Warne, 4th ed, 1974.

H. Mellanby, *Animal Life in Freshwater,* Chapman & Hall, 1975.

G. Thompson, J. Coldrey and G. Bernard, *The Pond,* Collins, 1984

Water Plants

H. Belcher and E. Swale, *The Beginner's Guide to Freshwater Algae,* H.M. Stationery Office, 1976.

S. Haslam, C. Sinker and P. Wolseley, *British Water Plants,* Field Studies reprint, E. W. Classey, 1975.

Flatworms

T. B. Reynoldson, *A Key to the British species of Freshwater Triclads,* Freshwater Biological Association: Scientific Publication No 23, 1978.

Rotifers

J. Donner, *Rotifers,* Frederick Warne, 1966 (only available in libraries).

Annelids

R. O. Brinkhurst, *A Guide for the Identification of Aquatic Oligochaeta,* F.B.A. Scientific Publication No 22, 1971.

J. M. Elliott and K. H. Mann, *A Key to the British Freshwater Leeches,* F.B.A. Scientific Publication No 40, 1979.

Crustaceans

T. Gledhill, D. W. Sutcliffe and W. D. Williams, *Key to British Freshwater Crustacea: Malacostraca,* F.B.A. Scientific Publication No 32, 1976.

J. P. Harding and W. A. Smith, *A Key to the British Freshwater Cyclopid and Calanoid Copepods,* F.B.A. Scientific Publication No 18, 1974.

D. J. Scourfield and J. P. Harding, *Key to the British Species of Freshwater Cladocera with notes on their Ecology,* F.B.A. Scientific Publication No 5, 1966.

Dragonflies

P. S. Corbet, C. Longfield and N. W. Moore, *Dragonflies,* Collins, 1960.

R. Merritt, *The Dragonflies of Great Britain and Ireland,* Harley, 1983.

Stoneflies

H. B. N. Hynes, *A Key to the Adults and Nymphs of British Stoneflies,* F.B.A. Scientific Publication No 17, 1977.

Mayflies

D. E. Kimmins, *A Revised Key to the British Species of Ephemeroptera with keys to the genera of the nymphs,* F.B.A. Scientific Publication No 15, 1972.

Water bugs

T. T. Macan, *A Revised Key to the British Water Bugs,* F.B.A. Scientific Publication No 16, 1976.

Alderflies

J. M. Elliott, *A Key to the Larvae and Adults of British Freshwater Megaloptera and Neuroptera,* F.B.A. Scientific Publication No 35, 1977.

Caddis flies

N. E. Hickin, *Caddis Larvae,* Hutchinson, 1967.

Beetles

F. Balfour-Browne, *British Water Beetles,* 3 vols, Ray Society, 1940–58.

Two-winged flies

C. N. Colyer and C. O. Hammond, *Flies of the British Isles,* Frederick Warne, 1968.

Spiders and Mites

C. D. Soar and W. Williamson, *British Hydracarina* (Water Mites), 3 vols, Ray Society, 1925–29.

Molluscs

A. E. Ellis, *British Freshwater Bivalve Molluscs,* Linnean Society Synopses of the British Fauna No 11, 1978.

T. T. Macan, *A Key to the British Fresh and Brackish Water Gastropods,* F.B.A. Scientific Publication No 13, 1977.

Vertebrates

T. B. Bagenal, *Observer's Book of Freshwater Fishes,* Frederick Warne, 1978.

D. Frazer, *Reptiles and Amphibians in Britain* (New Naturalist series), Collins, 1980.

INDEX

Illustration numbers are set in **bold** type

184

Key to the commoner aquatic animals

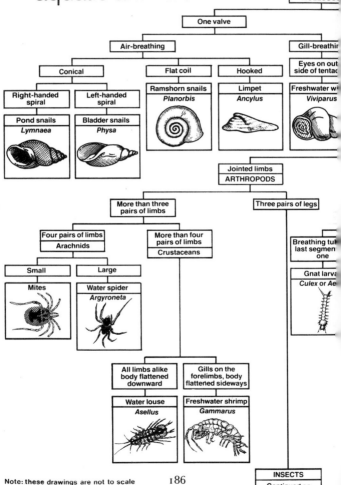

With shells
MOLLUSCS

One valve

Air-breathing

Conical

Right-handed spiral

Left-handed spiral

Pond snails
Lymnaea

Bladder snails
Physa

Flat coil

Ramshorn snails
Planorbis

Hooked

Limpet
Ancylus

Gill-breathing

Eyes on outside of tentacle

Freshwater winkle
Viviparus

Jointed limbs
ARTHROPODS

More than three pairs of limbs

Four pairs of limbs
Arachnids

Small

Mites

Large

Water spider
Argyroneta

More than four pairs of limbs
Crustaceans

All limbs alike body flattened downward

Water louse
Asellus

Gills on the forelimbs, body flattened sideways

Freshwater shrimp
Gammarus

Three pairs of legs

Breathing tube last segment one

Gnat larva
Culex or *Ae...*

INSECTS
Continued on page 188

Note: these drawings are not to scale

186

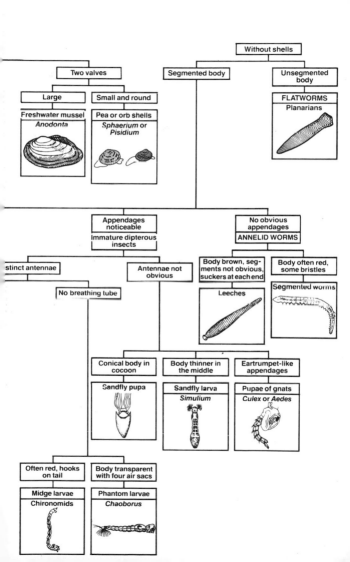

Without shells

Two valves

Large

Freshwater mussel
Anodonta

Small and round

Pea or orb shells
Sphaerium or
Pisidium

Segmented body

Unsegmented body

FLATWORMS
Planarians

Appendages noticeable
Immature dipterous insects

No obvious appendages
ANNELID WORMS

Body brown, segments not obvious, suckers at each end

Leeches

Body often red, some bristles

Segmented worms

...stinct antennae

Antennae not obvious

No breathing tube

Conical body in cocoon

Sandfly pupa

Body thinner in the middle

Sandfly larva
Simulium

Eartrumpet-like appendages

Pupae of gnats
Culex or *Aedes*

Often red, hooks on tail

Midge larvae
Chironomids

Body transparent with four air sacs

Phantom larvae
Chaoborus

459

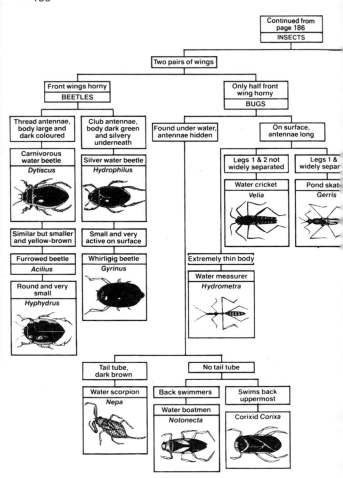

Continued from page 186

INSECTS

Two pairs of wings

Front wings horny
BEETLES

Only half front wing horny
BUGS

Thread antennae, body large and dark coloured

Carnivorous water beetle
Dytiscus

Club antennae, body dark green and silvery underneath

Silver water beetle
Hydrophilus

Found under water, antennae hidden

On surface, antennae long

Legs 1 & 2 not widely separated

Water cricket
Velia

Legs 1 & [2] widely separ[ated]

Pond skat[er]
Gerris

Similar but smaller and yellow-brown

Furrowed beetle
Acilius

Round and very small
Hyphydrus

Small and very active on surface

Whirligig beetle
Gyrinus

Extremely thin body

Water measurer
Hydrometra

Tail tube, dark brown

Water scorpion
Nepa

No tail tube

Back swimmers

Water boatmen
Notonecta

Swims back uppermost

Corixid *Corixa*

10mm 20 30 40 50 60 70 80

Scale for measuring specimens

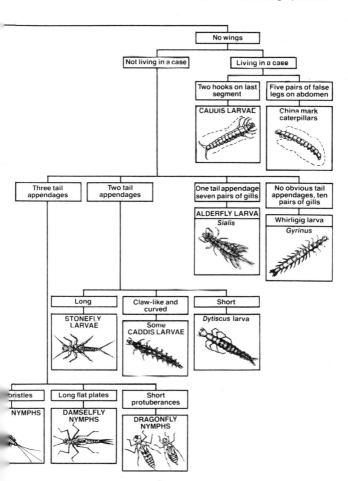